cleansepurifyenergize

cleansepurifyenergize

Sensible Detox Strategies to Improve Your Whole Health

Charmaine Yabsley

Foreword by Alison Shore Gaines
Holistic educator and coach, Kripalu Center and Omega Institute

Published in the USA and Canada by Sellers Publishing, Inc.
P.O. Box 818, Portland, Maine 04104
For ordering information:
(800) 625-3386 toll free
(800) 772-6814 fax
Visit our Web site: www.rsvp.com • E-mail: rsp@rsvp.com

Conceived and produced by
Elwin Street Productions
144 Liverpool Road
London N1 1LA
United Kingdom
www.elwinstreet.com

Cover design by Heather Zschock
Layouts designed by Louise Leffler

ISBN 13: 978-1-4162-0513-5
Library of Congress Control Number: 2008923439

10 9 8 7 6 5 4 3 2 1

Printed and bound in Singapore

contents

foreword

by Alison Shore Gaines

Cleansing, detoxing, fasting, purifying—whatever you call it, the practice of removing accumulated waste from your body is enjoying a popular resurgence now. A time-honored and natural method to enhance physical, mental, and spiritual well-being, fasting, in one form or another, is incorporated in all of the major religions and by health spas throughout world.

Since the 1970s, I have explored many methods of cleansing. In my personal quest to resolve carbohydrate cravings, environmental sensitivities, and migraine headaches, I experimented with raw juice fasts, lemon water cleanses, rice mono-diets, raw and live foods, herbal remedies, macrobiotics, Ayurveda, and more. Each method of cleansing has merits and one can certainly get benefits from any of them.

As my body purified and became more balanced, my symptoms disappeared. With continued cleansing, my relationship with food became easier, more enjoyable, and less conflicted.

Over the years, I studied with the pioneers of the natural foods movement: Deepak Chopra, Michio Kuchi , Annemarie Colbin, Gabriel Cousens, and many others. These diverse experts in Ayurveda, macrobiotics, and raw foods all espouse the profound effect diet and detox methodologies have on our physical, emotional, and spiritual well being.

I came to understand that there is no one diet or cleanse that fits all people all of the time. Purification practices can vary from taking in nothing at all, to a detox of water or lemon water only, to fresh fruit and vegetable juices, smoothies, grains, soups, and diets that include animal protein, and many more. Since 1988, I have guided thousands of people through my Purification Retreats and continually observe that some people experience best results with simpler methods and others need more complex carbohydrates and/or protein for optimal balance.

This book, *Cleanse, Purify, Energize*, offers a well-rounded, sensible cleansing approach for those who are non-vegetarian or are detox novices who want to improve their health by clearing sugar, caffeine, trans-fats, alcohol and/or nicotine from their system. The author offers a clear understanding of the detox process, delectable recipes, and energizing practices. With its beautiful presentation and personable manner, this book is such a delight to read that one feels inspired to follow the suggestions without delay! This is a thoroughly enjoyable, uplifting manual for an effective purification and a vibrant lifestyle beyond.

Alison Shore Gaines teaches her popular Purification Retreats at Kripalu Center, Lenox, Massachusetts, Omega Institute, Rheinbeck, New York, and other centers. The former chef/owner of a natural foods luncheonette and juice bar, Alison's Restaurant, Alison is a Holistic Health Educator, Nutrition Consultant, and Vibrant Life Coach with a private practice in Pittsfield, Massachusetts. She can be reached at asgaines07@aol.com or www.sacrednourishment.com.

detox basics

What does detox mean?

So you've decided to follow a detox plan. But do you know what detox actually means, and how to begin? Well, congratulations! Without even knowing it, your body has been detoxifying every day since you were born. To put it simply, detoxing is your body's way of eliminating toxins from its system. It does this quite easily, through body excretions, sweat, tears, and the breath. Your body has its very own built-in detoxification tools, which means that you're actually detoxing even while you're reading this.

Your detox system

	WHAT IT DOES	OVERLOAD	AT-A-GLANCE TEST
THE LIVER	The liver performs many different roles and processes around 75 percent of your body's waste products. Harmful toxins that cannot be absorbed are neutralized to become water-soluble before being absorbed by the kidneys or bowel.	If you drink too much alcohol, you won't feel the effects until two-thirds of your liver has been damaged. A high-protein diet puts a strain on the liver—as can regular use of headache remedies (such as paracetemol) and antibiotics.	Your liver is taking the brunt of too many late nights and take-out meals if your skin has erupted in spots, your breath smells, or your tongue is constantly coated with a white film. (See page 49 for further information on liver detox.)
THE KIDNEYS	Kidneys separate toxins and waste products, depositing them in the urine.	Eating too much salt places undue pressure on the kidneys. It's important to drink at least 3 pints (1.5 liters) of filtered water a day to flush out toxins and reduce the risk of kidney stones.	If you have pain in your lower back—on either side of your spine— or you're constantly tired, no matter how many hours of sleep you've had, then your kidneys may be suffering from overload.
SKIN	Skin is the body's largest organ, with a weight of around 6 ½ pounds (3 kg). Since your skin envelops your internal organs, it makes sense that a large amount of toxins are excreted through it.	Too many toxins can be a strain on your skin's excretion process.	If your skin is dry, scaly, or you have broken out in spots (especially around the T-zone area of your face), then it is likely that your skin is suffering from toxin overload.
LUNGS	Every day our lungs are expected to filter out the nasties from our environment, whether it's pollution, cigarette smoke, exhaust fumes, or other airborne toxins.	A polluted environment and poor breathing techniques can reduce the lungs' ability to oxygenate blood and remove carbon dioxide if our lungs aren't exercised to their full capacity.	If you're having trouble taking deep breaths, and you live on a busy road, or you live with a smoker, then your lungs could certainly do with a clean.
LYMPHATIC SYSTEM	The lymphatic system is necessary for our overall good health.	An underperforming lymphatic system can no longer deal with illness or infection.	You may have spots along your chin line or dark circles under your eyes no matter how well you've slept.
INTESTINES AND BOWEL	The nutrients from the food we swallow are absorbed into the small intestine. Any excess or waste is then passed through the colon.	Ensuring your bowels function correctly is necessary for long-term health. A sluggish bowel can form cancer-causing substances.	You may notice spots on your chin or have a bloated stomach, even first thing in the morning.

Eliminate, exercise, energize

Implementing a detox program for yourself is slightly different than merely relying on your body to do its normal, daily routine. A proper detox involves a program of Eliminating (particularly all your favorite, naughty foods), Exercising, and Energizing. A detox program, particularly one specifically tailored to your individual needs, is the best, and quickest, way to ensure that you're eliminating the toxins that are overloading your system.

Eliminating

Cutting out foods that are causing your body to become sluggish or unhealthy is the first step toward detoxing. And not just detoxing. Eliminating junk foods, caffeine, sugars, and processed foods is a great start to a healthier way of eating and living for the future. Elimination doesn't mean cutting out *everything*—just the products that are causing your body ill health.

Exercising

A detox diet tailored especially for you will only benefit from some gentle exercise. Slow, gentle movements such as walking, swimming, yoga, pilates, or tai chi, are all ideal to help your body relax and rejuvenate. (Read more about exercise plans on pages 21–22 and 82–85).

Energizing

Detoxing is going to help you lose weight, tone up, and put a sparkle back into your eyes, but the most immediate health benefit you'll notice is a boost in energy levels. This is because your body is potentially so exhausted from constantly processing toxins (or trying to), that it has run out of steam.

Yes, you'll feel tired at first. In fact you'll probably feel more tired than you did before. But this is because your body is going through a withdrawal process and is craving its usual energy boosters, such as sugar, nicotine, alcohol, or white carbohydrates. The good news though is that it doesn't take very long to eliminate these from your system, and you'll notice the energy boosting benefits within days.

Who needs to detox?

According to scientists, nobody needs to detox, as our bodies do it naturally. Yet according to health professionals, everybody should detox at least once a year. So who's telling the truth? Well, in their own way, both camps are. In an ideal world, we would all eat a full and varied diet of organic foods; we would exercise daily; have a massage every week; and we would avoid pollution, cigarette smoke, and stress.

Unfortunately, we're not all saints (thank goodness!) so it stands to reason that our bodies all need a good rest from unhealthy diet, pressures, and environment. You are the only person who can say whether you need a detox. Check the list below for any symptoms that you experience regularly and then decide:

- bad breath
- frequent burning sensation when you urinate
- fullness in stomach
- difficulty digesting fatty foods
- flatulence or bloating or excessive belching
- diarrhea
- irregular bowel movements
- recurrent headaches
- sensitivity to chemicals, pollution, cigarette smoke, perfumes
- spots or acne
- poor tolerance of alcohol

If you suffer from any of the above regularly, your body may not be digesting or detoxifying properly. It's advisable that you reserve some time for yourself and your health to get it back on track. The various detox systems in this book will help you.

When to detox

Ideally, your detox should take place when you have the time to prepare the specific foods you need and also when you'll have the space to rest. Pick a weekend when you are alone or, if you have children, get your partner or a family member to take them out for the day, or even for an overnight stay. Remember, this detox is all about you.

For longer detoxes, again, begin on a weekend if possible (or when you have two successive days with few, or no demands on you). It goes without saying that trying to detox during the Holiday party season is almost impossible, as are the sunny days of summer.

PLANNING YOUR DETOX

- Set a goal for yourself. If you really want to fit into that bikini, then set your detox for at least three weeks before your vacation, not the day before.

- Avoid beginning a detox on a Monday.

- If you're detoxing on the weekend, mark out the time in your calendar and treat this time as you would an appointment with a friend—one you wouldn't cancel.

- Turn off your cell phone, turn on the answering machine, and make sure you have all the ingredients you need so that you won't have to venture out.

- Tell friends and family that you're detoxing so that they know not to offer you a glass of wine or a slice of chocolate cake.

How to get started

You've already made the first step and decided that you're going to detox, so now what?

First, decide what type of detox is best for you. This book contains five detox plans, plus some beauty and home detox programs so you can look and feel your glowing best.

Each detox plan contains a daily schedule to follow. You'll also discover that detoxing isn't about depriving yourself, it's about treating your body to the tastiest, healthiest foods and treatments. Each detox contains tasty recipes to ensure that you won't be reaching for the cookie jar.

Before going on a detox, you should be medically fit and neither pregnant nor on any medication. Check with your family doctor before beginning any diet, detox, or exercise regime.

Now let's get started!

Body basics

The intestines are integral to your overall health and well-being. Along with your bowels they filter out toxins and harmful products from your stomach before sending them to your liver to be processed. Your bowels excrete processed toxins (feces)—but if they are sluggish, toxins can remain there for longer than is healthy for your body.

Inner cleansing

Ideally, you'll have one bowel movement a day, and your feces should be solid and dark brown. If they're sloppy or pellet-shaped, or if they contain blood or other forms, then it's likely that you're constipated or your bowels aren't functioning correctly. Check with your family doctor immediately for medical advice.

By cleansing your intestines, you're actually revving up your body's internal engine to increase its productivity and effectiveness. Luckily, our bodies are hardy machines, and it doesn't take very long to cleanse our systems, and return to optimum health.

Your liver. . .

Since you're reading a book about cleansing, detoxifying, and energizing your body, we should discuss your body's anatomy and its various functions.

The main focus is your liver: I'm sure you've woken up after a few heavy nights on the run with a pain in your side (and a splitting headache, but that's another story!). Well, that's your liver's way of telling you to spend a few nights in watching TV and eating steamed vegetables.

When it comes to your health, your liver is like the engine of a car. If you don't keep it in good condition, your body just won't run properly. And like a car, keeping your liver healthy all comes down to what you put in it.

The liver sits to the right of the abdomen. It is one of the largest organs in your body and one of the most important. It's main job is to filter and detoxify substances within your body: food, nutrients, liquids, and oxygen. Keeping your liver healthy really is just as important as maintaining a healthy heart.

. . . and how it works

The liver is divided into a large right lobe, subdivided into three sections, and a smaller left lobe that tapers towards a tip, which is in contact with the stomach, intestines, and esophagus.

Unlike any other organ, the liver has a double blood supply. Oxygenated blood from the heart to the liver, which needs about a quarter of the heart's total output, comes via the hepatic artery. This subdivides into many branches within the liver to provide oxygen to all its cells.

The portal vein also feeds the liver with blood. It carries nutrients from digested food such as fats and glucose from the intestines and spleen, which the liver either uses or stores depending on the body's needs.

All the liver's blood drains into the hepatic veins. Bile, which assists digestion by processing fats in the small intestine and neutralizing stomach acid, leaves the liver through a network of tiny bile ducts. These fuse to form the right and left hepatic ducts, which themselves fuse and carry bile to the gallbladder.

WHAT THE LIVER DOES

- It aids digestion by helping the absorption of fat and vitamins.

- It distributes nutrients in food.

- It helps to cleanse the blood by removing toxins.

- It produces important proteins for the blood, notably albumin (which regulates the exchange of water between blood and tissues) and complement (which plays a part in the immune system).

- It provides coagulation factors essential for clotting blood after injury.

- It supplies globin, a constituent of oxygen-carrying hemoglobin in the blood.

- It makes cholesterol and proteins that help carry energy-supplying fats around the body.

- It stores glucose that the body does not need immediately in the form of glycogen, which it converts back to glucose and releases into the bloodstream when needed.

- It regulates the blood level of amino acids, chemicals that are the building blocks of proteins.

- It protects the body by removing bacteria and neutralizing toxins that would otherwise accumulate.

- It filters many chemical substances and waste products from the blood.

- It secretes up to 2 ½ pints (1.14 liters) of bile daily which remove waste products—food and water contain thousands of non-nutrients that require constant liver processing and detoxification.

- It banks vitamins A, B, D, E, K, and others for release into the bloodstream when supplies get low.

- It helps to retire old blood cells.

- It turns sugars and fats into protein, and vice-versa, maintaining the blood sugar level.

- It regenerates itself by creating new cells as old or damaged ones die off.

HOW TO MAINTAIN A HEALTHY LIVER

The liver largely looks after itself and suffers little wear and tear. Drinking in moderation is the main preventive measure for liver disease. Complete abstinence from alcohol is the only way of improving the function of a drink-damaged liver.

FOODS AND YOUR LIVER

If you have avoided eating fats because you have been scared of putting on weight, then you may have been doing yourself more harm than good. Fats are actually essential to a healthy, balanced diet.

Fat has always been given bad press. The word alone conjures up negativity: cellulite, obesity, and heart problems. But, recent research has shown that eating too little fat may mean that you're putting yourself at risk of the very health problems you've been trying to avoid.

This is not an excuse to overdo the potato chips and chocolates! Fats fall into two categories, those that are good for you and those that are not. The ones associated with ill health, such as obesity, heart disease, and cancer, are saturated fats. They tend to be solid at room temperature, and include butter, lard, and fatty cuts of red meat. The fats found in these foods need to be processed through the liver and can overload it, meaning the liver has very little time or energy to process other toxins, such as pollution and pesticides. Ideally, you should consume no more than approximately ¾ ounce (20 g) of saturated fat a day (this is easily achieved by following a balanced diet, so you won't have to deprive yourself of too many tasty foods).

The good fats that bring plenty of health benefits are called unsaturated fats—monounsaturates and polyunsaturates. These fats are liquid at room temperature and are mostly found in vegetable sources, particularly vegetable oils, but also in foods such as chicken, fish, and nuts. These foods and oils are healthy as they supply essential fatty acids that cannot be manufactured by our bodies. Essential fatty acids help maintain cell structure, lock in the skin's moisture, and are required in the production of the hormone-like substances called prostaglandins that regulate the menstrual cycle, reproduction, and blood pressure.

By cutting out fats from your diet, your body suffers in several ways. A deficiency of fats can manifest itself in dry or scaly skin, lowered libido, depression, or behavioral problems. Too little fat may also make it harder for you to lose weight. Essential fatty acids help burn stored fat by assisting in the transport of fat-burning oxygen to the body's tissues.

When choosing the fats in your diet, it's important to include the right types:

Omega-6 fats: belong to the polyunsaturated fat family and eating them can help lower cholesterol
Sources: nuts, seeds, and vegetable oils
Monounsaturated fats: help lower cholesterol and can improve the balance between "good" and "bad" fats
Sources: olive oil, avocados, nuts, and rapeseed and groundnut oil are other good sources
Omega-3 fats: Research has shown that we should eat proportionally more of these polyunsaturates and less of the omega-6 type
Sources: oily fish, including herring, mackerel, salmon, and flax seed

Exercise: sweat it out

The benefits of regular exercise are numerous. Exercise builds muscle, burns fat, makes the heart and lungs work more efficiently, lowers the density of damaging sugars in the blood, and is a major factor in preventing osteoporosis. Best of all and probably most importantly, exercise makes you look and feel better, since it releases endorphins—brain mood-elevating compounds.

Ironically, it's when you most feel like hibernating and snuggling up on the sofa that your body benefits the most from getting up and moving. It doesn't necessarily matter what sort of exercise you do, as long as you get your body moving and your heart rate pumping, your mind and your body will reap the benefits.

Exercising while detoxing is imperative—you really can't do one without the other. Exercise supports the detoxification process, as it strengthens the immune system, encourages the elimination of toxins, and, most importantly, gives you energy.

Which exercises should I do?

There are no rules on what exercises you should or shouldn't do when you're detoxing, although you probably won't feel like completing a marathon during a seven-day detox. But certainly during a month-long detox you should incorporate at least three sessions of aerobic activity into each week; a shorter detox will benefit from slower exercise such as walking, yoga, or tai chi.

STRETCHING

What it is: Stretching your body to maintain its flexibility is probably the most underrated part of anybody's exercise program. While stretching should not constitute the entire workout, it's important to allow the connective tissue surrounding your muscle fibers to lengthen, thereby allowing your body to support more vigorous activity.

Types: Yoga, pilates, relaxation classes.

Why you should do it: If your body is tense you may find that you're "holding in" extra weight—such as that spare tire around your middle that no amount of dieting or exercise can shift. This is because tense muscles hold natural toxins such as lactic acid and ammonia: when you relax, the toxins are released so they can be absorbed into the bloodstream.

How often: Ideally do some form of stretching every day—first thing in the morning and last thing at night will help to release toxins from your body.

AEROBIC EXERCISE

What it is: Aerobic exercise is any large muscle activity that you can sustain for 2 to 3 minutes or longer. The word aerobic means "with oxygen," as this form of exercise requires oxygen from the air reaches your muscles.

Types: walking, gardening, hiking, bicycling, lap swimming, jogging, or cross-country skiing.

Why you should do it: During a hard 60-minute workout you can sweat out as much as 2 pints (1 liter) of water, 1 percent of which is toxins. The more you exercise, the more toxins you lose. Once your body is moving regularly your bowels will do the same. Constipation and irregular bowel movements are indicators of an overloaded system, yet exercise can increase the rate at which the bowel processes matter by up to 60 percent. Best of all, regular exercise will help you lose weight and tone up. Weight loss on crash diets (which I do not endorse) leads to the sudden release of toxins into your system, which your body can't handle. If you exercise regularly in tandem with following a healthy, balanced eating plan, then once you start burning more calories than you're taking in, your body will start to release fat for energy.

How often: Any aerobic exercise should be performed for 20 to 60 minutes at least five times a week. Research shows that people who exercise on a regular basis have lower levels of stress than their fellow couch potatoes. Remember that when beginning an exercise program you should take it slowly and steadily. Too much too fast, and your body will be unable to handle the number of free radicals that are released into its system, and you may find that you come down with an uncommon amount of colds and illnesses.

RESISTANCE EXERCISE OR STRENGTH TRAINING

What it is: Strength training increases muscle strength and mass, bone strength, and your body's metabolism.

Types: free weights, weight machines, callisthenics, and resistance training.

Why you should do it: Working up a real sweat with boxing, kettlebells, or weights is not only a fantastic way to tone up and lose weight quickly (see workouts on pages 82–85), but you'll be increasing the intensity of detoxification several times over.

How often: At least twice a week, for 20 minutes at a time.

YOGA AND OTHER EASTERN EXERCISES

What it is: In the past decade, yoga and other forms of Eastern-style exercise have increased in popularity. Many who were happiest pounding the treadmill at their local gym or running around the park, have traded in their running shoes for a yoga mat and deep breathing. Yoga and other mind/body exercises are the ideal accompaniment to a detoxifying program— particularly ones that are conducted in short bursts (such as a 1-day or 48-hour detox). There are many forms of yoga, so try a few different classes to find which one suits you.

Types: Hatha, Vinyasa, Ashtanga, power yoga, Iyengar, Kundalini, Bikram/Hot yoga, tai chi, pilates.

Why you should do it: Yoga, dance, tai chi, and pilates are all excellent forms of gentle exercise when detoxing and should be incorporated into your weekly exercise schedule. You'll find that you'll not only benefit physically from this, but mentally as well.

How often: Yoga should be done around three times a week, though during a detox program this should be increased to at least once a day, as it helps to relax and balance your body while eliminating stress and toxins.

detox foods

A non-toxic diet

Eliminating toxins from your diet and eating only healthy, natural, organic foods is both harder and easier than you think. It's more difficult because in order to live a non-toxic life you need to be constantly aware of what you're putting in your mouth. However, it's much easier, because even the supposedly naughty toxins (such as alcohol and coffee) can be drunk in healthy quantities. There are also organic options of most foods available to you.

Living a toxin-free lifestyle does take some time and consideration. It's more than just ordering your food through an organic grocer or buying non-toxic healthcare products. But in the end you'll feel so much better, that it will all be worth it.

Having seen which toxins to avoid (page 13), a healthier lifestyle is now just a matter of replacing your bad habits with good ones. For instance, if you love Chinese take-out, learn to cook your favorite dishes yourself: that way you'll be sure of the ingredients. You are also likely to prepare smaller portions, and so be less likely to overeat and exceed your recommended daily calorie intake. Having fresh, wholesome ingredients on hand goes a long way to ensure that you follow a healthy, toxic-free diet and lifestyle.

How important is a non-toxic diet?

While it is possible to exist on ready-meals, non-organic fruit and vegetables, and never do a detox, do you really want to live such a dull life when the alternative is glorious technicolor? An organic, toxic-free lifestyle gives you a greater chance of:

- living longer
- avoiding diseases such as heart problems, cancer, respiratory illnesses, and kidney or liver problems
- having more energy
- recovering more quickly from colds and flu
- being more positive

Of course, it's not necessary for you to throw everything you own in the trash and start over with brand-new, non-toxic products. The secret to non-toxic living is choosing what *really* makes a difference and getting by with those products that don't. That way you'll spend your hard-earned money on foods that really make a difference to your health, and not waste your money on ones that make little or no difference to your toxic levels.

Even organic foods need washing, and non-organic food should definitely be washed before eating or preparation to remove any lingering traces of pesticide. Remember, that just because a product is labeled "organic" this doesn't mean it's good for you. An "organic" can of soda still contains additives and sugar, albeit a little less than its toxic counterparts, but it is still an unhealthy option.

According to the British Soil Association (BSA), it's not completely necessary for all your foods to be organic but those that should ideally be organic are shown in the list on this page.

Elsewhere in the home, I'd highly recommend you go organic for the products in the list. Not only are they healthier for you, but they are kinder to the environment, recyclable, and have less chance of causing irritation to the skin.

✳ ORGANIC FOODS

- Bread
- Milk
- Meat
- Cheese
- All vegetables (especially peppers, spinach, potatoes)
- Fruit (particularly ones without an outer layer or skin that you have to peel, such as strawberries, cherries, apples, peaches, or blackberries)
- All salad ingredients, such as lettuce and spinach

✳ ORGANIC HOUSEHOLD ITEMS

- Detergents
- Dish-washing liquid
- Hand soap
- Beauty products (many beauty products contain cancer-causing or allergy-related ingredients)
- Paint, particularly if you or your family have breathing problems

Herbs and supplements

How herbs help you detox

Herbs, those plants in your garden that you probably promised yourself you'd cook with and use every day, aren't just there to look pretty. They're packed full of nutrients—each herb contains detoxifying and health-giving properties that no self-respecting health convert should live without. Here are the top ten herbs that you should definitely cultivate and cook with in the future.

PARSLEY

Parsley is a bit of a star when it comes to its health and detox properties. Packed full of vitamin C, it's not only a natural breath freshener, but it's also a great way to support a detox. The flavonoids in parsley, such as luteolin, are powerful antioxidants that neutralize free radicals produced, for example, by pollution, and so help prevent damage to cells.

MINT

Cooling, calming, and refreshing, mint eases stomach and digestive problems, relaxes the mind and can ease headaches.

BASIL

Smelling a few leaves of basil can help relieve a tension or migraine headache, and it helps soothe menstrual symptoms. Adding basil to your meals can also help relieve stomach cramps and alleviate bloating, as it contains natural antispasmodic properties.

BAY

This dried leaf from the Bay Laurel tree is often used in spicy soups and curries, but its medicinal benefits are also plentiful. Bay leaves contain laurenolide, an energizing ingredient, so it's a good element to include in a longer-term detox.

GARLIC

Garlic is packed full of goodness. Many people take garlic to ease cold and flu symptoms, but its benefits are even more far-reaching. It can improve circulation, enhancing the flow of nutrients and oxygen to the fingers and toes. Its cold-deflecting abilities derive from its sulfurous compounds that help the body resist infections. These compounds also stimulate the liver and act as a detoxifier, helping rid the body of any toxins.

CILANTRO

Cilantro seed has a number of medicinal uses. It's used as an antibacterial and a treatment for colic, neuralgia, and rheumatism, plus it contains chlorophyll, so like parsley, neutralizes bad odors—good news for those suffering from bad breath.

GINGER

Ideal for stimulating the digestive system, it's just the ingredient you need to add to your tea or cooking, particularly if you're feeling bloated or suffering from digestive problems.

DANDELION

Dandelion extracts salt and water from the kidney. This is ideal if you have been suffering from water retention (squeeze your ankle bone to see if there's excess fluid around it as a quick test). It contains potassium, one of the best forms of diuretic and one that isn't evident in over-the-counter diuretics.

How supplements can help you detox

In an ideal world, we would eat healthy, fresh, organic food three times a day, with balanced, nutritious snacks morning and afternoon. But then we would also be strong, balanced, and relaxed from the hour's exercise we managed to fit in as a part of our laid-back, stress-free life. Of course, this is just a dream. Nobody is really able to live like this.

Supplements are there to do what they say: supplement your diet with any nutrients you may be missing out on. In no way are supplements meant to replace meals or vital ingredients—but research has found that around 42 percent of us take one or more supplements each day.

It has been acknowledged by the *Journal of the American Medical Association* that the taking of supplements has a positive effect on your health. Researchers concluded that those individuals whose vitamin intake is below the recommended level are more prone to developing diseases such as cancer, heart disease, and osteoporosis, and there have been successive positive studies that demonstrate the disease-prevention benefits that result from taking nutritional supplements.

As part of your detox, it will be necessary to support your program with some supplements. The following vitamins and minerals have been chosen specifically because they help to support the body's natural detoxification process, not because they replace it.

Recommended supplements

SUPPLEMENT	DESCRIPTION	QUANTITY
CO ENZYME Q10	Needed by your body's enzymes to assist them in the activities in the cells for the body, such as helping with energy production. It's particularly supportive of the liver, as it helps to break down toxins.	30–300 mg per day
MILK THISTLE	A natural hangover cure, milk thistle is one of 30 supplements that can help to support and strengthen the liver's function. Trials have shown that taking milk thistle in supplement or tincture form can help the liver process toxins more easily. It also helps the body speed up the detoxification process, so toxins remain in the body for a shorter length of time.	1 x standardized extract capsule or tablet three times a day Or 10 ml tincture in hot water
GINSENG	Ginseng may help to improve energy levels (even sexually): a rather wonderful supplement to include in your daily health plan.	2–3 capsules between meals or 1 cup of ginseng tea or 5–10 g powder in liquid
CHLORELLA	Made from algae, chlorella is a high source of protein and vitamins. It includes antioxidants A, C, and E, and chlorophyll, which increases the oxygen in the blood. It has been championed for its ability to attach itself to particular toxins, which means that it grabs hold of toxins such as heavy metals and excretes them.	100 mg two to three times per day
VITAMIN C	The most widely taken of all the supplements, vitamin C is essential for the production of healthy collagen (the stuff that holds your skin together), helps the white blood cells fight infection, and helps to heal wounds. It is also an antioxidant, so it joins in the fight against free radicals such as pollution and cigarette smoke.	2000 mg per day To help your body absorb vitamin C, you should take the supplement with a glass of orange juice
ECHINACEA	This wonder product accounts for around 10 percent of all health product sales. Echinacea is believed to help fight colds, flu, and other viruses, as well as boosting the immune system.	2–3 g supplement 15 drops of tincture three times a day
MSM	Methylsulfonylmethane (MSM) is a naturally occurring sulfur compound found in small quantities in the body and in food. It helps in the maintenance of bones, joints, and ligaments and can either be taken separately or as part of a blend.	1000 mg three times a day
ALOE VERA	One of the richest medical and nutritional plants, it has 20 minerals, 18 amino acids, and 12 vitamins. Aloe Vera extract is proven to be beneficial to the immune system and digestive system.	Follow dosage suggestions on label

Detox drinks

Juicing your fruits and vegetables is a great addition to your detox plan. Not only is juice an easier way to get lots of vitamins and nutrients into your body, but the liquid form makes it easier for your body's organs to process.

Almost all fruits and vegetables can be juiced; there are no strict rules to follow (just remember to remove seeds or pips first). Experiment with various ingredients and mixtures—who knows, you may come up with a winning combination!

One point to remember is that juicing fruit and vegetables can remove some of the fiber from your diet (unless you use a masticating juicer, which presses, rather than pulps the fruit). It is therefore important that you add fiber to your diet, whether through foods such as beans, wholegrains, or cereals, or through adding a fiber supplement to your daily diet or to the juice.

Why you should eat five a day

Five portions of fruit and vegetables per day may be the antidote to many illnesses and diseases, yet many of us still struggle to factor fruit and vegetables into our diet. Juicing is an easy way of achieving the recommended amount, especially if you find the prospect of five portions a day rather daunting.

There are certain fruits and vegetables that are particularly good for detoxing.

APPLE

We all know the saying "an apple a day keeps the doctor away," and it does seem to help. Apples have a laxative effect on your body because they contain pectin that encourages excretion of certain metals. Ideal if you've been overdoing the potato chips and candy, as pectin helps to remove food additives.

PEAR

Pears are a useful and tasty fruit. If you're diabetic, pears, like apples, are a good stable snack to have as they do not contribute to big increases in blood sugar levels. This is because the fruit does not require large amounts of insulin for digestion. For this reason also, pears are an excellent food to enjoy if you are on a weight loss diet as the very slow rise in blood sugar levels means you are less likely to overeat. And being packed full of fiber, they give your stomach the impression of being full, which also means you're less likely to overindulge.

BANANA

If you are having stomach problems, try eating a banana. Ripe, they can be eaten to treat constipation. Unripe, they are an excellent way to stop diarrhea. They are also an ideal late-afternoon snack, as their ½ ounce (20 g) fruit-sugar content is quickly absorbed into the bloodstream, giving an almost immediate increase in energy. They help you feel fuller for longer, and the extra energy is ideal during the early days of your detox. Great if you suffer from fluid retention.

TIP

If you suffer from insomnia, try eating a banana about 30 minutes before going to bed. Ripe bananas may raise mood and help you go to sleep. They're believed to have a soothing effect on the body by stimulating serotonin.

WATERCRESS

This leafy vegetable is packed full of vitamins and is an ideal addition to your detox. Recent research by scientists at the Institute for Food Research in Norwich, UK, found eating watercress triggers a protective reaction against cancer.

ACAI BERRIES (PRONOUNCED AH-SAH-EE)

Acai, a purple wonder-berry with twice the cancer-beating antioxidants of blueberries, has been found to destroy four-fifths of cancer cells. In addition they have the health-giving omega-6 and omega-9 fatty acids (rarely found in fruit) are low in calories, and contain fiber, calcium, and vitamins.

KIWI FRUIT

This lovely sweet fruit contains high levels of vitamin C. Indeed, eating just one kiwi fruit a day supplies you with your recommended daily intake of this vitamin.

POMEGRANATE

The juice from the pomegranate is one of nature's most powerful antioxidants. In addition to vitamin C, pomegranates contain a group of antioxidants called flavonoids. This large group of plant chemicals has a wide range of beneficial actions, including anti-inflammatories, antibacterial, and antivirals. Their most important effect is as antioxidants, which guard your body against free radicals, the harmful molecules formed by natural metabolic processes in the body, and by pollution and cigarette smoke.

GINGER

Ginger contains extracts called bilobides that improve the tone and elasticity of blood vessels, and so promote healthy circulation and improve the transport of vital nutrients around the body.

CARROTS

Not just for rabbits, carrots contain high levels of the antioxidants alpha- and beta-carotene, which can help the body guard against cancers. Carrots can also help to increase circulation in the body, so they are an ideal juice to enjoy when starting an exercise program.

WATERMELON

Watermelon—and watermelon juice—is the tastiest, most thirst quenching treat you can have on a summer's day (yes, even more so than a cold beer!). The vibrant red color of watermelon is caused by the phytochemical lycopene—a substance also present in tomatoes—that may help protect the body against cancer. Watermelon also contains high levels of vitamin C, good for supporting the body during the detoxification process. As this fruit has such a high water content it is ideal for keeping the skin well hydrated, and ensuring it stays smooth and supple.

GRAPEFRUIT

The dieter's favorite food. Grapefruit really does deserve its reputation as the miracle weight loss fruit. According to recent research, you can lose weight simply by adding grapefruit to your normal meals, without changing any other eating habits. It is believed that the enzymes in grapefruit allow the body to burn sugar rather than store it as fat. You should also feel more energetic after enjoying grapefruit for breakfast, as the body uses the nutrients purely for energy purposes.

BEETS

The beautiful, bright red color of beet juice isn't just attractive to the eye, it's great for the waistline. Beets have been used over the centuries as folk remedies for anemia, menstrual problems, and kidney disorders. This root vegetable contains betacyanin, which, along with its other antioxidants, have been shown to enhance detoxing processes in the liver.

AVOCADO

If people avoid avocados because they are fattening, then they are missing out on a treat: not just in taste, but health-wise too. High in fiber, protein, and vitamin E, they also contain glutathione, an antioxidant that fights free radicals. Avocados help to dissolve toxins, particularly ones caused by alcohol.

ASPARAGUS

Asparagus contains an amino acid called asparagine, which, along with its high potassium content and low sodium, makes it a diuretic and a cleanser, useful for processing proteins and flushing through the kidneys. Diuretics help reduce both blood pressure and water retention in the legs.

BROCCOLI AND KALE

Broccoli contains at least 50 percent more vitamin C than oranges, and kale is rated as one of the highest antioxidant foods. Both are an excellent source of fiber, which helps keep the bowels working efficiently and feeds the good bacteria. Broccoli and kale are rich sources of sulfur-containing chemicals called glucosinolates, which have powerful actions in the detoxification processes in the liver.

ARTICHOKES

The globe artichoke is best known, medicinally, for supporting the liver and gallbladder, and is a useful tool in boosting detoxification and digestion. Artichokes help relieve the symptoms of irritable bowel syndrome such as nausea, pain, constipation, and gas. Herbalists recommend artichoke for helping relieve water retention and high blood pressure.

ALFALFA AND MUNG SPROUTS

Amongst the easiest foods to grow yourself, alfalfa and mung sprouts are essential for detoxification. They contain a fiber called plantix, which helps to digest food additives within the system.

And don't forget…

WATER

Water truly is nature's very own first aid kit. While you can survive for up to a month without food, you could only survive for about three days without water. The body is 75 percent water, yet you only need to drink around 3 pints (1.5 liters) each day to keep your body well supplied. You need water to flush toxins through your liver and kidney, to help pump oxygen through your body, and to keep your skin smooth and supple.

TIP

If you're tired in the afternoon, you may well be dehydrated. Instead of reaching for a sugary snack to boost your energy levels, pour yourself a glass of room temperature water. You'll immediately feel the rejuvenating effects.

Drink recipes

Now that you know what a wonderful effect fruit and vegetables can have on your health, here are a few recipes for you to try, from the multi-vitamin boost of the ultimate health juice to the sublime feel-good smoothie, there is a drink for every occasion and they are all delicious!

All recipes serve one unless otherwise stated.

✳ THE LEMON AID JUICE

Why it works: This drink gives the liver a kick-start to cleanse your toxin-filled body. Your bowels will also appreciate the gentle nudge into action.

This is a sharp-tasting drink containing vitamins A and C, selenium and zinc, nutrients that will help replace those lost through burning the candle at both ends and give you energy to start your day. This drink also has a high volume of water, which should sort out any dehydration and accompanying pounding headache.

½ grapefruit
1 kiwi fruit
½ lemon
large slice pineapple
½ cup (60 g) frozen cranberries
½ cup (60 g) frozen raspberries

Juice the grapefruit, kiwi, lemon, and pineapple. Blend with the frozen berries. Drink immediately.

✳ THE MIRACLE JUICE

Why it works: This juice is packed full of iron and vitamins B and C: it will start to undo all the damage you've caused to your system over the past few months.

1 beet
1 carrot
¼ inch (6 mm) ginger root
1 apple
1 pear

Juice ingredients together and drink immediately.

✳ MORNING GLORY

Why it works: As the ultimate health juice, it contains more than your day's requirements of vitamins A, B, C, and E. It will also ward off the hunger pains too, as it is very filling; so you'll be less likely to stop for an egg and bacon sandwich on your way to work.

1 apple
1 pear
1 carrot
1 stick of celery
1 kiwi fruit
¼ inch (6 mm) ginger root

Juice all the ingredients together. Leave in the refrigerator for 15 minutes to chill if desired, or just add ice. For extra sweetness put the mixture in a blender and add a banana and a handful of blueberries.

STRAWBERRY STAR

Why it works: Strawberries can help banish the stains caused by red wine and nicotine, so try this juice after a big night out.

5 strawberries, hulls removed
handful of blueberries
handful of raspberries
1 banana
1 tbsp yogurt
handful of pumpkin and sunflower seeds
1 ¾ cups (425 ml) apple juice (freshly juiced
    or 100 percent pure fruit juice)

Combine all ingredients in a blender. Blend until seeds are completely mixed in. Pour into tall glass, add ice if desired.

BANANA SMOOTHIE

Why it works: This juice is packed full of vitamin B and natural sugars and will give you a feeling of well-being, while the nutmeg will help to boost your mood.

1 banana
1 tsp honey (preferably organic or Manuka)
shaved nutmeg
1 ¼ cups (280 ml) skim or dairy-free milk

Put all the ingredients into a blender and mix thoroughly. Pour into a glass, with ice if preferred, and add more nutmeg to taste.

IRON STEIN

Why it works: Iron is necessary for several brain functions: it helps to transport the blood around the body, thereby oxygenating the gray matter.

handful of blackcurrants
¼ mango
1 banana
1 kiwi fruit
1 orange
thyme

Put all the ingredients into a blender and mix thoroughly. Pour into a glass, add ice if desired.

SOOTHER SMOOTHER

Why it works: This drink is high in water content and is therefore an ideal way to boost your hydration levels—great if you're feeling tired or you have a headache.

1 apple
1 pear
1 slice watermelon
1 papaya
star anise

Juice ingredients together and drink immediately.

GLASS OF BUBBLY

Why it works: Acai berry and pomegranate juice are credited with containing the highest amount of antioxidants of all the fruits. Antioxidants are needed to fight off the effects of pollution, smoke, fats, and general 21st-century living.

⅔ cup (150 ml) acai berry juice
⅔ cup (150 ml) pomegranate juice
⅓ cup (100 ml) mineral water
crushed ice

Blend all ingredients together. Garnish with mint to taste.

detox plans

24-hour detox

You may think that you won't be able to achieve many health benefits in just 24 hours, but during this time your body will go through regeneration, cleansing, and resting—it just needs you to take the time to pamper it.

This is a liquid only day—don't worry, you won't go hungry, but if you do then make some miso soup from a packet. Ban the following today:

- ready-cooked meals
- fried food
- high fat foods
- salt and sugar
- chocolate
- tea
- coffee
- alcohol
- cigarettes

Why you need this detox

☐ You've drunk alcohol more than three nights in a row

☐ You've been under pressure at work (which has now finished)

☐ You feel constantly on the verge of getting a cold

☐ You feel slightly bloated

☐ You're constipated

☐ You want to fit into that special outfit on the weekend

What you'll need

First of all, if you decide you want to have a solitary detox day, you need to ensure that you can't and won't be interrupted. Resist all temptation, turn off your cell phone and, if possible, switch your telephone to direct voicemail. Don't turn on the television or computer—today is purely for relaxation and calm. Switch the radio to a classical or relaxation music station—or stockpile your favorite, soothing CDs.

Create an oasis in just one room of your home: your bedroom, living room, or even your bathroom if it's large enough.

Prepare some liquids for your day. If you get bored with water, add lemon, lime, strawberries, or mint leaves for taste and variety. Stock up with herbal teas as well. Try peppermint, licorice, or green tea—these are good for digestion and are calming as well.

Stock up on candles, tealights, essential oils, or incense sticks for a relaxing ambience.

Wear whatever you like. Whether it's your favorite pajamas and slippers, or your sweat pants and oldest T-shirt, it doesn't matter as long as you're comfortable.

Your detox day shopping list:

- strawberries
- bananas
- celery
- ginger
- carrots
- apples
- pears
- oranges
- beets
- nutmeg
- blueberries
- raspberries
- dandelion or nettle tea
- acai berries
- dairy-free organic milk
- organic natural yogurt
- organic muesli
- seeds (such as pumpkin and sunflower seeds)
- ginger root
- honey (preferably organic or Manuka)
- milk thistle supplement
- fresh mint leaves
- tealights
- essential oils (such as grapeseed, peppermint, chamomile, lavender, juniper, grapefruit)
- grapefruit essential oils
- Dead Sea salts or Epsom salts

Your detox day

7:22 AM

Yes, we know it's early, but we're here to kick-start your health program. This is the perfect physical time to wake up—researchers at the University of Westminster, London, have found that people who rise between 5:22 and 7:21 AM have higher levels of the stress hormone cortisol in their bloodstream. So set your alarm for 7:22 AM safe in the knowledge that you'll be well rested and relaxed.

7:30 AM

Drink a glass of room temperature, filtered water. This will replace fluids lost during the night, and it will help your kidneys to function at optimum level.

7:34 AM

Get your detoxification started with a massage. Mix 1 tsp almond oil with 1 tbsp grapeseed or olive oil and 10 drops of peppermint oil. Apply to your stomach in a clockwise direction until your hand is above your leg. Then stroke down along your thigh. This aids digestion and relieves blockages.

8:00 AM

Don't get out of bed straightaway: stretch your body from head to toe for a gentle wake up. Now it's time to get up. Head to the bathroom. Take a dry body brush and use it in sweeping movements from your toes all the way to your shoulders. Always brush towards your heart, as this will help to boost circulation, and, in turn, banish dry skin and cellulite. Set the water to lukewarm—not too hot, nor too cold—wash your hair and use an envigorating body scrub all over. Towel dry and apply your favorite scented moisturizer, all over.

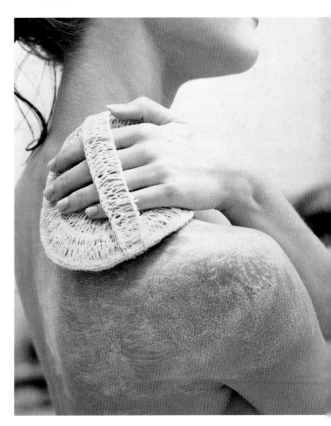

8:30 AM

Time for breakfast. Try this great juice, it will fill you up and get your digestive system started.

✳ **SUN UP SMOOTHIE**

1 apple
1 pear
1 carrot
½ beet
1 banana
organic muesli

Juice the first four ingredients together, then pour the mixture into a blender. In the blender, add some ice, one banana, and a handful of organic muesli. Blend until smooth. Drink immediately. Take a milk thistle supplement as a part of today's detox program.

9:00 AM

Put on your comfy workout gear and head to the local park for a brisk hour's walk. While walking doesn't burn as many calories as running, research has shown that it has just as many (if not more) health and emotional benefits. Walking can help lift depression, encourage creativity (also known as walking meditation), and tone the butt, stomach, and thighs.

10:30 AM

Today is all about cleansing, so try some suitable recipes. The following ingredients are renowned for their detoxifying properties, plus you'll feel nice and full, so you won't think you're depriving yourself.

✳ DETOX DAY DRINK

¼ inch (6 mm) ginger root
1 stick celery
1 carrot
1 apple
1 pear

Juice all ingredients together. Store in refrigerator to cool, or add ice if required. Drinking the mixture at room temperature is just as tasty.

11:00 AM

Time to do nothing. Today is all about you, so make some time for yourself to do ab-so-lute-ly nothing. If you have a garden, position yourself in the sunshine and just close your eyes and clear your mind. If you don't have outside space, then find your favorite spot in the house and just spend 60 minutes doing nothing. It's harder than it sounds!

12 NOON

If your energy levels are flagging, it's a great time to enjoy some natural fruit sugars with this lip smackin' smoothie.

TIP

If you are finding it difficult to spend an hour doing nothing, why not plan your next vacation? This is your time so you can be as fanciful as you like. Let your imagination wander and before you know it the hour will be over and you will have had a wonderful adventure just using the power of your own mind.

✳ BANANA SMOOTHIE

Why it works: Ideal for any time of the day, this juice is packed full of vitamin B and natural sugars. It will give you a feeling of well-being, whatever time you drink it.

1 banana
1 tsp honey (preferably organic or Manuka)
shaved nutmeg
1¼ cups (280 ml) dairy-free organic milk or
    almond, oat, or rice milk

Put all the ingredients into a blender and mix until the banana is completely broken down. Pour in a glass (with ice if preferred) and add more nutmeg to taste.

1:00 PM

It's been a busy day, so it's time for your nap. Just an hour's sleep during the day can be highly beneficial for your health. According to research, it can make you thinner, happier, less stressed, and lower your blood pressure. This is the time of day that the pineal gland releases a small amount of sleep-inducing hormone melatonin, which causes lethargy. So head to your bedroom, throw a comfy blanket over you, and head off to the land of nod. Don't forget to set your alarm first, otherwise you may sleep the day away!

2:00 PM

Time to wake up your brain and body. Drink a glass of water before rising. Then, head back to your local park for a yoga workout, or if you'd rather not Salute the Sun in public, to your living room. Put a yoga instructional DVD on and follow the program for a top-to-toe easy wake up routine.

3:00 PM

✳ **FILL 'ER UP RECIPE**

4 oranges
handful of acai berries, blueberries,
    raspberries, and strawberries combined
organic natural yogurt (optional)

Juice oranges and add to the blender. Add the
berries and organic natural yogurt if you like and
blend until smooth. Pour over ice in a tall glass
and sip slowly.

3:30 PM

It's pampering hour. Apply a face mask and use
this relaxing time to give yourself a manicure and
pedicure. Or lie down with some of your favorite
magazines or a book and let the mask do its work.

4:30 PM

You've done really well and hopefully you're feeling
the positive effects of your detox day. Time for a
warming drink. Place fresh mint leaves into a teapot
and add boiling water. Leave for a few minutes, then
pour a cup of refreshing, cleansing, mint tea.

5:30 PM

Wash off your face mask, then run yourself a warm
aromatic bath for further relaxation time.

✳ **AROMATIC BATH**

10 drops grapefruit essential oil
10 drops juniper essential oil
1 cup Dead Sea salts or Epsom salts

Mix the essential oils with the salts before
pouring into a tub of warm water. Turn up
the music, light some candles, and immerse

yourself fully in the bath. Enjoy the warmth
and aroma for at least 20 minutes before
getting out and drying yourself from head
to toe.

Apply some body moisturizer and put on some
comfortable pajamas. If your hair is wet, dry it
fully, but don't bother about styling it. Scatter
a few drops of chamomile or lavender oil on
your pillow and bedsheets and make yourself
a cup of chamomile tea.

7:00 PM

Time to wind down from the day, so try to avoid any
fruits as they contain high levels of natural sugars.
An ideal end of day juice should involve vegetables
with a deeper, earthy flavor.

✳ **ON THE BEET**

1 beet
1 carrot
1 pear
1 stick of celery
pumpkin seeds (optional)
sunflower seeds (optional)

Juice ingredients together. Add pumpkin seeds
and sunflower seeds for an extra iron boost.

9:00 PM

It's early, but it's time to hop into bed. Listen to some
music or read for about 20 minutes before turning off
the light. Enjoy a restful night's sleep and look forward
to a new, revitalized you tomorrow morning!

3-day liver detox

The liver is the main detoxification tool of the body. Giving it a bit of help every now and then is the kindest thing you can do.

Liver detox

As we learned on page 13, an overloaded liver can lead to numerous health problems. Helping it out could be the best thing you can do for your health today, tomorrow, and the future. Nutritionist Natalie Savona recommends completing the following checklist to find out if your liver is in need of detoxification:

Why you need this detox

- ☐ Your skin looks sluggish and gray
- ☐ Your tongue is coated with a white, furry substance
- ☐ The whites of your eyes are bloodshot or tinged with yellow
- ☐ You've been suffering from spots
- ☐ You wake up exhausted, no matter how many hours of sleep you've gotten
- ☐ Your bowel movements are sluggish or painful
- ☐ Your urine smells strongly and/or is orange in color
- ☐ You find it difficult to focus or concentrate for long periods of time
- ☐ You feel listless, and have little interest in anything new

- Have just two to three moderate servings of protein foods a day. These include milk, meat, poultry, fish, soy, and legumes.
- Eat vitamin C- and E-rich foods, such as oranges, berries, kiwi fruit, peppers, dark green vegetables, and wheat germ. They help to protect the liver from potentially damaging free radicals.
- Try green tea. Also rich in antioxidants, it may enhance the effects of vitamins C and E.
- Take milk thistle supplements. Extracts of the plant protect liver cells, encourage repair of damaged cells, and stimulate growth of new cells.
- Use dandelion coffee or root infusions. When combined with milk thistle, they speed up the flow of cell-damaging toxins away from the liver.

BREAKFAST

* **EVERYDAY MORNING JUICE**

1 grapefruit
1 lemon
2 tbsp extra virgin olive oil
1 clove garlic, crushed
1 inch (2.5 cm) ginger root, grated

Juice together and drink every morning.

Day One
LUNCH

* **POTATO AND ARTICHOKE SALAD**

Artichokes are the ideal liver cleansers, so this is great for helping the body's elimination process.

10 cups (1 kg) baby new potatoes
⅓ cup (80 ml) walnut oil
2 tbsp white wine vinegar
2 tbsp Dijon mustard
salt and freshly ground black pepper
1 cup (100 g) thinly sliced red onion
2 x 2 ⅔ cups (285 g) marinated artichoke
    pieces, drained

Cook potatoes in boiling salted water for 15 minutes or until tender. Drain well. Cool, then cut potatoes in half. Whisk oil, vinegar, and mustard in a bowl. Season to taste with salt and pepper. Combine potatoes, onion, artichokes, and dressing in a bowl. Serves 6 to 8.

DINNER

✳ **BABY SPINACH AND RADICCHIO SALAD**

Both ingredients are highly recommended for boosting the performance of the liver.

1 large radicchio lettuce
5 cups (250 g) baby spinach
1/3 cup (40 g) pine nuts, toasted
sea salt flakes

For the dressing:
1/3 cup (40 g) raisins
1/3 cup (80 ml) extra virgin olive oil
2 tbsp red wine vinegar

Combine raisins, oil, and vinegar in a jar; shake well. Allow to stand for 1 hour. Wash and dry the lettuce and spinach leaves. Just before serving, toss pine nuts and add dressing and sea salt to taste through the combined salad leaves. Serves 2.

Day Two
LUNCH

✳ **VEGETABLE RICE PAPER ROLLS WITH CHILI DIPPING SAUCE**

This recipe is packed with nutrients to lower cholesterol and encourage digestion.

1/2 cup (50 g) vermicelli noodles
2 medium avocados
1 medium carrot
1 bunch chives
24 small round rice paper wrappers
3 red radishes, grated
2/3 cup (80 g) bean sprouts, trimmed
24 large mint leaves

Chili Dipping Sauce
1/2 cup (125 ml) white vinegar
2 tbsp Manuka honey (to taste)
1 tsp salt
1/4 cup (60 ml) water
1 clove garlic, crushed
1/3 cup (40 g) finely chopped red onion
1/2 cup (60 g) deseeded, finely chopped
    cucumber
1 tbsp chopped fresh cilantro
1 small fresh red chili, chopped
1 tbsp cashews, toasted, chopped

Directions for sauce: Bring vinegar, honey, salt, and water to a boil in a medium saucepan, and boil, uncovered for 2 minutes. Pour vinegar mixture over remaining ingredients in a medium bowl. Allow to cool.

Place vermicelli noodles in a bowl of hot water for 2 minutes or until softened. Drain well. Thinly slice the avocados. Cut the carrot into long, thin strips. Cut chives the same length as the carrots. Cover a board with a damp tea towel. Place one sheet of rice paper in a bowl of warm water until softened. Place on tea towel, top with a slice of avocado, some of the carrot, radish, sprouts, a mint leaf, some chives, then add noodles to the center of the sheet. Fold bottom half of the rice paper up. Fold in one side, roll over to enclose the filling. Repeat with remaining rice paper sheets and remaining ingredients. Place the rolls on a plastic wrap-lined tray, cover with a damp paper towel, and refrigerate until you're ready to serve.

Serve with Chili Dipping Sauce. Makes 24.

DINNER

✳ VEGETARIAN FLAN

Packed full of vitamins and nutrients this will support your immune system, which may be feeling the effects of the detox.

2 tbsp olive oil

2 zucchini, thickly sliced

1 red pepper, cored and sliced

1 red onion, peeled

1 cup (100 g) rice flour

pinch of salt

⅔ cup (75 g) soy margarine

⅔ cup (75 g) sun-dried tomatoes

1 tbsp Dijon mustard

⅔ cup (75 g) dairy-free cheese, grated

2 organic, free-range eggs, beaten

scant ½ cup (100 ml) soy organic milk or
    almond, oat, or rice milk

2 tbsp fresh chives

Preheat the oven to 400°F (200°C). Pour olive oil into roasting pan, and heat in oven. Add vegetables. Roast for 30 minutes. Meanwhile sift flour and salt into a bowl. Rub in margarine until it resembles breadcrumbs. Stir in 3 to 4 tablespoons of water and knead until dough is smooth. Chill for 20 minutes. Take vegetables out of oven. Add tomatoes. Stir and leave to cool. Reduce oven to 375°F (190°C). Roll out dough and place in an 8-inch (20-cm) fluted flan pan. Place parchment paper and dry beans over the top of the pastry (this stops the pastry from rising unevenly). Bake for 10 minutes. Remove beans and paper and bake for 5 minutes. Spread the mustard over the pastry case and sprinkle with cheese. Arrange cooked vegetables on top. Beat together remaining ingredients and pour over the top. Bake for 30 to 40 minutes. Serves 4.

Day Three
LUNCH

✳ **CHICKEN SALAD WITH SOY DRESSING**

An average serving of chicken provides you with more than half your daily requirement of protein. The accompanying vegetables in this salad are filled with energy-giving vitamins.

1 tbsp peanut oil
4 chicken breast fillets
4 cups (400 g) shredded Chinese cabbage
4 green onions, sliced
1 stick celery, diced
½ cup (50 g) snow pea sprouts

For the dressing:
4 tbsp (60 ml) peanut oil
2 tbsp soy sauce
1 tsp soy sesame oil
1 tsp grated fresh ginger
1 clove garlic, crushed
2 tbsp lime juice

Heat oil in frying pan. Cook chicken until browned on both sides and cooked through. Slice thinly. Combine chicken, cabbage, onion, and celery in bowl. To make the dressing, combine all ingredients together in a bowl and mix well. Top the salad with sprouts and drizzle with the dressing. Serves 4.

DINNER

✳ **STEAMED LEMONGRASS CHICKEN AND RICE ROLLS**

If you're feeling stressed, tired, or have the blues, this easy-to-make recipe is filled with mood-boosting ingredients.

4 stalks lemongrass, halved lengthwise
3 chicken breast fillets, halved lengthwise
1 tsp sesame oil
2 red chilies, deseeded and chopped
1 bunch *gai larn* (Chinese broccoli), halved
3 cups (300 g) plain rice noodle rolls
soy sauce and lime wedges to serve

Place the lemongrass in the base of a bamboo steamer. Top with the chicken and then brush the chicken with the sesame oil and sprinkle with chili. Cover the steamer and place it over a saucepan of boiling water to steam for 3 minutes. While the chicken is steaming, place the *gai larn* and rice rolls in another bamboo steamer of the same size. Place this second steamer on top of the chicken steamer and cover. Steam for a further 5 minutes or until the chicken and *gai larn* are tender. Serve with small bowls of soy sauce and wedges of lime. Serves 4.

3-day total detox

If you don't have the time (or think you don't have the willpower) for a month-long or even week-long detox, then an extended weekend break could be the answer for you. Try to combine this 3-day detox with some of the detoxifying beauty treatments (see page 96) for a pure body detox experience.

Why you need this detox

- [ ] You've been burning the candle at both ends
- [ ] You've got parties/weddings/celebrations coming up
- [ ] You want to lose those last few pounds
- [ ] Your skin is blotchy and spotty
- [ ] You've been suffering from insomnia
- [ ] You haven't been to bed before midnight for at least a week
- [ ] Your shoulders are tense
- [ ] You can't remember the last time you cooked a healthy meal for yourself
- [ ] You can't remember the last time you went for three days without alcohol

A three-day detox won't completely clear your system of toxins, nor will you lose a load of weight in those 72 hours, but you will feel more energized, rested, and rejuvenated. More importantly, you should rediscover your enthusiasm for all things healthy, to help you on your way to adopting a more wholesome lifestyle.

Foods to cut out	Foods to include
Dairy	Vegetables
Meat	Fish
Alcohol	Fruit
Sugar	Water
White carbohydrates	Herbal teas
Packaged/fast foods	

The most important element of this 3-day detox is ensuring you have all the peace, space, and calm that you need. Cancel all arrangements (perhaps tell people you're going away for the weekend) and turn your phone off.

- Read through the menus on the following pages and stock up on your ingredients.

- Book yourself a massage or make sure you have the ingredients for a relaxing aromatherapy bath.

- Line up some DVDs to watch.

- Make sure you have plenty of good books to read.

- Get ahold of your local gym's schedule and circle one or two classes you'd like to attend. Then sign up. Choose a relaxation or stretching/yoga class. This isn't the time to get all hot and sweaty.

- Ensure you have all your beauty treatments on hand if you don't want to spend money on a facial (or see page 100 for a DIY facial treatment).

- Make sure your favorite, most comfy pajamas are clean, and change the sheets on your bed to your favorite covers.

- Stock up on tealights and candles.

- If you smoke or have been drinking excessively (even coffee), try to plan ahead by cutting down prior to your detox or giving up completely. Replace your coffee with decaffeinated blends, use nicotine patches if you really can't give up cigarettes, and try to have an alcohol-free night at least the night before you begin.

- Kitchen appliances: steamer, juicer, and blender are all used in the recipes for your detox.

Day one

Rise and shine! It's day one of your detox and you need to get off on the right foot. Get up at your usual weekday time (even if it's a weekend)—that way you can fit in as much good living today as possible.

Time for your warm water and lemon juice to help kick-start your liver. After 8 hours or so without water, you're probably dehydrated. You should aim to drink at least 3 pints (1.5 liters) of filtered water before lunchtime.

BREAKFAST

If you're feeling a little fuzzy headed, it's a sure sign that your liver is underperforming. Try this detox juice that's guaranteed to put a zing in your step.

✳ **MOVING ON UP**

Ultra green juice that helps to maintain energy levels and enthusiasm for life.

1 cup (100 g) broccoli
¾ cup (100 g) chopped kale
1 cup (40 g) parsley
1 apple
2 sticks celery

Juice and serve in a tall glass.

PORRIDGE WITH MIXED FRUIT

A serving of oats per day will help to stabilize blood sugar levels. If you're trying to give up smoking, then porridge could help, as it's believed to help fight cravings.

1 cup (100 g) halved apricots
1 cup (100 g) raspberries
1 cup (100 g) pitted, halved prunes
2 ½ cups (225 g) oatmeal
filtered water

Place the fruits in a bowl, as you would a fruit salad, and combine. Place the oatmeal in a saucepan, cover with plenty of water, and bring to a boil. Simmer for 5–10 minutes, stirring constantly, until thickened. Pour into a bowl and top with fruits.

EXERCISE

After breakfast it's time to get moving. Put on your sweat pants and sneakers and head out for a brisk walk around the block. Even if it's cold, wet, and windy, the fresh air will do you good. While you walk concentrate on your breathing and just placing your feet firmly on the ground. This will help to calm your mind and banish all stresses and worries.

TIP

Take some time to do what you never have time for: absolutely nothing! Whether it's sitting in the garden or lying on your bed, try to spend at least 30 minutes doing nothing. Just half an hour will help rest your mind, relax your muscles, and get you in the zone.

MID-MORNING SNACK

A handful of prunes or dried apricots will help to flush out your bowels. This has two advantages: you'll feel and look lighter because you won't be so bloated; and if your bowels are working regularly, then your skin (particularly around your chin) will be clearer and smoother.

DETOX TASKS

Try decluttering your home. Just focus on one room (or even a drawer) and have a good clear out. Bag up any clothing you haven't worn for the past 12 months and take it to your local thrift store or list it on www.freecycle.org.

LUNCH

PEA AND BROAD BEAN SOUP

This is a perfect recipe for keeping your kidneys healthy. Peas are also a good source of vitamin C, as well as supplying iron, carotenes, and B vitamins—necessary for a healthy nervous system.

2 ¼ cups (225 g) frozen peas
2 ¼ cups (225 g) frozen fava beans
3 ¾ cups (900 ml) vegetable stock
salt and freshly ground black pepper
harissa paste

Place the peas, beans, and stock in a large saucepan and bring to a boil. Cover and simmer for 30 minutes, or until the vegetables are tender. Pour into a food processor or blender and blend until smooth. Pour back into the pan and heat through. Season. To serve, spoon a little harissa paste over each bowl of soup.

AFTERNOON SNACK

Another handful of dried fruit or nuts to fill you up and provide you with essential fatty acids.

DINNER

✳ LIME, TOMATO, AND SCALLOP SALAD

Limes are high in vitamin C, and, served with scallops, this salad provides all the nutrients needed to energize you.

2 ½ cups (250 g) rice noodles
5 cups (500 g) scallops
1 tbsp sweet chili sauce
1 tbsp lime juice
2 ½ cups (250 g) trimmed, chopped asparagus
3 ⅓ cups (330 g) halved cherry tomatoes
¼ cup (25 g) flaked almonds, toasted

For the dressing:
½ cup (125 ml) peanut oil
2 tbsp fresh cilantro, chopped
1 tbsp fresh mint leaves, chopped
2 small fresh red chilies, deseeded, quartered
¼ cup (60 ml) lime juice

Place noodles in large heatproof bowl, cover with boiling water and leave for a couple of minutes until just tender; drain. Rinse under cold water and drain. Broil the scallops in batches. Combine chili sauce and lime juice and brush the scallops as they cook. Steam asparagus until just tender, rinse under cold water, then drain. To make the dressing, combine all of the ingredients together in a bowl and mix well. Gently toss noodles, scallops, and asparagus in a large bowl with the tomatoes and the dressing. Sprinkle with almonds. Serves 4.

PRE-BEDTIME TREAT

If you feel the beginnings of a headache (and you may if you've gone without cigarettes, coffee, and alcohol), then it's time to speed up your detoxification process, while supporting your system. Turn back to page 46 for the comforting Aromatic Bath. Just add a few drops of rose or jasmine essential oil for an extra beauty boost.

Day Two

You may feel a little groggy this morning, and you may even have a few spots if you've been burning the candle at both ends recently. Don't worry, this is actually a sign that your body is detoxifying. Using the Dry Skin brushing technique on page 96, give yourself an early morning all over wake-up treatment before jumping into a lukewarm shower. Wash and condition your hair before putting on some comfy clothes.

BREAKFAST

✳ ENERGY BOOSTER

This is high in silicon and potassium—ideal if you suffer from energy slumps or leg cramps (especially at night).

1 medium parsnip
1 green pepper
small bunch watercress
½ cucumber
1 tbsp mint to garnish, chopped

Juice ingredients together and serve over ice with a sprinkling of mint.

✳ SMOOTH AND SWEET HONEY AND BERRIES

The World Health Organization (WHO) recommends honey as an ideal remedy for stomach upsets and it is also a great skin healer. I highly recommend Manuka honey, which can help aid digestion and has even been recommended for treating certain strains of MRSA (Staph infection). Added to berries, which are high in antioxidants, this morning starter is a sweet and tasty way to start the day.

4 slices gluten-free bread
4 tbsp natural organic yogurt (plus a little extra
    for spreading onto toast)
6–8 tbsp uncooked Manuka honey
finely grated rind of ½ lemon
¾ cup (75 g) blueberries and raspberries
½ tsp grated nutmeg

Toast the bread until golden brown. Mix yogurt and honey together along with the lemon rind. Spread a small amount of honey onto the toast, followed by a layer of the yogurt mixture. Scatter the berries over the top, followed by another drizzling of honey. Grate the nutmeg on top.

EXERCISE

It's time to do some stretching. Either go to a local yoga class, or put on a yoga DVD and follow the instructions. Make sure you perform the movements on a yoga mat or adequately padded flooring so that you don't hurt yourself.

LUNCH

✳ **ITALIAN SALAD**

This tasty salad has the added weight-loss benefits of apricots, which also provide slow-release energy into your system.

1 cup (100 g) dried apricots, sliced
2 ¼ cups (225 g) asparagus tips
4 ½ cups (450 g) new potatoes, sliced
4 slices Parma ham
1 head lettuce
1 cup (100 g) sundried tomatoes

For the dressing:
3 tbsp olive oil
4 tbsp balsamic vinegar
2 tbsp honey (organic if possible)
salt and freshly ground black pepper

Whisk dressing ingredients in a bowl. Add apricots and marinate for 30 minutes. Meanwhile, cook asparagus tips in a pan of boiling salted water for 5 minutes, until tender. Drain and rinse under cold water. Boil new potatoes in salted water for 10–15 minutes until tender. Drain and allow to cool. Cut the Parma ham into pieces. Wash the lettuce. Arrange the lettuce leaves on a platter and top with sliced potatoes, asparagus tips, ham, and tomatoes. Scatter apricots and dress just before serving.

DETOX TASK

Use this quiet time for contemplation. Grab a pen and clean sheet of paper and write down five goals you'd like to achieve during the next four weeks. Don't be vague though. Instead of writing: "Lose 5 pounds," be specific about how you would achieve this. For example, "Lose 5 pounds by walking in the park for 30 minutes after work every day." You'll be more likely to stick to a plan when you've already worked out the logistics. Try clarifying five goals you'd like to address from various areas of your life.

AFTERNOON SNACK

Spread some wheat-free crackers with peanut butter or hummus for an energy lift. Avoid any fatty spreads, such as butter or cheese.

EVENING MEAL

✳ **FISH IN SLEEPING BAGS**

This is a quick and easy way to increase your levels of essential fatty acids. Add some herbs to the recipe to aid digestion.

olive oil
4x 7 oz (400 g) sole fillets
juice of 1 lemon
4 tomatoes, thinly sliced
1 lemon, peeled and thinly sliced
sea salt and pepper
2 peppers, cored, deseeded, and thinly sliced
1 tbsp cilantro
1 tbsp parsley
14 oz (400 g) baby new potatoes
1 ⅓ cups (200 g) runner beans

Lay a large sheet of foil on a baking tray and preheat oven to 425°F (220°C). Pour a thin layer of olive oil over the fillets, followed by lemon juice. Place tomato and lemon slices on the fillets adding salt and pepper as desired. Add peppers to the fillets. Fold sides of foil to meet in the middle and roll to close, until fish are completely covered. Place in oven and bake for 20 minutes. Meanwhile, place the potatoes and beans into boiling water and boil for 8–10 minutes, or until slightly soft when cut by a knife. Add the herbs to the fish, drain the beans and potatoes, and serve. Serves 4.

Day Three
BREAKFAST

* **HEAD TO TOE**

A sharp drink full of vitamins A and C, selenium and zinc that'll energize you from the top of your head to the tip of your toes.

½ grapefruit
1 kiwi fruit
large slice pineapple
⅔ cup (60 g) frozen raspberries
⅔ cup (60 g) frozen cranberries
lime wedge

Juice the grapefruit, kiwi, and pineapple. Blend with the frozen berries. Throw in a lime wedge and serve with a thick straw.

* **FRUIT SALAD WITH YOGURT**

This is an ideal weekend recipe, as you have more time to prepare it, and it's a healthier alternative to cereal or a skillet breakfast.

4 strawberries, hulled
handful of blueberries
1 kiwi fruit, peeled and quartered
1 apple, cored and quartered
1 orange, peeled and sectioned
¼ melon, cut into small segments
2 tbsp (30 ml) organic yogurt
seeds (optional), such as sunflower or
  pumpkin seeds

Toss fruit in bowl, pour some organic yogurt over the top, and add seeds to taste.

EXERCISE

Get wet! Head to your local swimming pool and submerge yourself in water. It doesn't matter if you're not the fastest swimmer in the world or your style isn't up to Olympic standard. Spend at least 30 minutes swimming and alternate your speeds to give yourself a good cardiovascular workout. Then spend some time just floating on your back letting the water and your thoughts wash over you.

If your gym has a sauna or steam room spend at least 10–20 minutes relaxing in the heat. See page 108 for more on the health benefits of saunas.

LUNCH

* **THAI SWEET AND SOUR SOUP**

Prawns contain omega-3, required by the brain for optimum health.

4 cups (1 liter) fish stock
1 stalk lemongrass
2 limes
2 tbsp honey (organic if possible)
1 handful cilantro, chopped
5 cups (500 g) prawns, shelled

In a large saucepan gently heat the fish stock. Crush the lemongrass thoroughly. Mix the juice of the limes with the honey and lemongrass and heat gently with half the stock for 5 minutes. Remove the lemongrass and pour the honey mixture into the rest of the stock. Add three-quarters of the chopped cilantro. Simmer for 2 minutes, stirring continuously. Add the prawns and gently poach for 5 minutes. Add the remaining cilantro leaves when serving to taste.

DETOX TASK

Do nothing! That's right, your activity for this afternoon is to do absolutely nothing at all. Sit yourself in the garden or comfortably on your bed and just let your mind drift away. If you begin to focus on one particular thought, write down the topic for contemplation later, and return to letting your worries and thoughts wash over you like the ocean's waves.

DINNER

✳ SHREDDED BEET AND FETA SALAD

Beets have long been used to help purify the blood, you should also include them in your morning juice.

1 cup (100 g) golden raisins
2 medium zucchini
3 ½ cups (350 g) uncooked beets
2 medium carrots
1 endive lettuce
2 avocados
1 ¾ cups (175 g) soy feta cheese, crumbled

For the dressing
⅓ cup (90 ml) olive oil
1 tbsp (15 ml) Dijon mustard
grated rind and juice of 2 oranges
salt and freshly ground black pepper

Place the raisins in a bowl. Whisk together the dressing ingredients, pour over the raisins, and allow to soak for 30 minutes. Cut the zucchini into strips. Grate the beets and carrots. Wash the endive lettuce and separate into leaves. Halve the avocados, stone, peel, and cut into slices. Mix together the salad ingredients in a large bowl. Add the crumbled cheese. Add more salt and pepper if required. Drizzle the dressing over the salad and serve immediately.

Stop-smoking detox

If you're a slave to the cancerous white stick, but are reading this chapter because you're determined to give up, then congratulations! Giving up smoking is extremely difficult—some research says that nicotine is more addictive than heroin—and requires immense willpower and strength. This stop-smoking detox is designed to help quash nicotine cravings, as well as encourage the elimination of toxins from your system.

Why you need this detox

- [ ] You smoke (either socially or habitually)
- [ ] You no longer taste the flavors of food and drink
- [ ] Your emotions are constantly changing
- [ ] You're suffering from headaches, colds, and coughs more than ever
- [ ] You're determined to give up smoking forever

Worried about your weight?

For many people, weight gain after quitting smoking is a real concern. However, with a healthy, balanced diet and regular exercise (both of which will help expediate your post-nicotine recovery and alleviate cravings) you should keep your weight at its current level.

The detox food list

While I can't give you the willpower you'll need to stick to this stop-smoking plan, certain foods can help you resist the urge to light up. Alkaline foods, such as vegetables, fruits, and eggs, are highly recommended for people who are stopping smoking. This is because a high level of acid within your body will increase your desire and even need for a cigarette. Alkaline foods keep the nicotine in your system for longer, thus reducing your need for another "fix," so you'll be slowly detoxing, rather than going "cold turkey," which can be a shock to the system.

ALKALINE FOODS TO EAT
Vegetables: asparagus, alfalfa, zucchini, carrots, celery, spinach
Fruits: melon, mango, prunes, apricots, avocado, raisins, kiwi fruit (avoid blueberries and cranberries)
Other foods: oats, meat substitutes, such as tofu, soy products, quinoa, herb teas
Acidic foods to avoid: Meat, poultry, rice, dairy, and wheat products are all acid-forming, so avoid these as much as possible

Other stop-smoking aids
NICOTINE PATCHES
These work by providing your body with small amounts of nicotine throughout the day and night to help reduce cravings.

HYPNOTISM/NEURO LINGUISTIC PROGRAMMING (NLP)
This therapy works by recognizing your trigger points and helping "reprogram" your mind so that you'll no longer react the same way. Many people swear by hypnotherapy as a means to stop smoking, although you may need a few sessions.

CUTTING DOWN

Eliminating your morning cigarette is the first step in quitting for good. By cutting down your regular cigarette breaks (first thing in the morning, with a drink, on the way home from work), you've already removed the "habit factor" from smoking. Write down the five most common times of the day you have a cigarette and cut these out one week at a time. To make this easier, distract yourself with another (healthier) habit. For instance, if you usually have a cigarette first thing in the morning, spend that time making a nutritious, tasty juice (see recipes pages 37–39).

COLD TURKEY

This is possibly the hardest, but also the most effective way of quitting. Stopping smoking altogether is, according to experts, the only way to truly stop, and remain stopped. If you have decided to go cold turkey, then enlist the help of friends and family to support your decision, and follow the detox plan as closely as possible.

HEALTH BENEFITS

According to Action on Smoking and Health (ASH) almost 88 percent of people who smoke want to quit, mainly for health and financial reasons. It's never too late to give up—just consider these health benefits if you quit today:

TIME SINCE QUITTING	HEALTH BENEFITS
8 hours	Oxygen levels return to normal, circulation improves, and nicotine and carbon monoxide levels in blood reduce by half
24 hours	Carbon monoxide and nicotine are no longer in your body
48 hours	The ability to taste and smell improves
1 month	Your appearance improves. Skin loses its grayish pallor, becomes less dry, and has fewer wrinkles
3–9 months	Coughing and wheezing declines
1 year	Risk of a heart attack reduces by 50 percent compared to that of a smoker
10 years	Risk of lung cancers falls to about half that of a smoker
15 years	Risk of heart attack falls to the same as somebody who has never smoked

ALTERNATIVE REMEDY HELP

Susan Curtis, Medicines Director of Neal's Yard Remedies suggests the following alternative remedies for those giving up smoking.

- The homeopathic remedy Nux Vomica can ease irritability and support your central nervous system.

- St. John's Wort will counter the cravings and any natural feelings of being low or feeling depressed from the chemical withdrawal.

- Support your nervous system with Lemon Balm & Rose, either as a tea or, if you are not fond of tea, as a tincture. Just add a few drops to your drinking water.

- If you are having problems sleeping, Passiflora and Chamomile Tea, can help you with relaxation and sleep.

- If you have tried unsuccessfully to stop smoking, consider acupuncture. Research has shown acupuncture to be highly effective where other treatments may have failed in the past.

- Caladium 6c, another homeopathic remedy, is said to help quitters resist cravings.

- Lobelia can help support your lungs as they eliminate nicotine, but you should only use it with the advice of a qualified herbal practitioner.

TIP

Oats can help stop cravings when you're quitting, as they help calm the nervous system. Enjoy porridge for breakfast as often as you can. Or visit a nutritionist to discuss the use of Avena Sativa—oat juice—which will also help cleanse your body.

Detox program

It takes around three months to completely remove all traces of nicotine from your system, so it's important to get into a routine of the meals that follow. But remember, if it doesn't stick the first time, you can always try again.

Suggested meals

BREAKFAST

✳ FRESH FRUIT SALAD

2 kiwi fruit
2 bananas
3 oranges
2 apples
2 pears
6 strawberries
1 mango
flaxseeds, pumpkin seeds, and sunflower
seeds (optional)
honey (optional)
natural organic yogurt (optional)

Chop all fruit into small pieces or segments. Add to a large bowl and mix until the seeds, juices, and fruits run into each other. Add honey or natural yogurt if desired. Serves 2.

✳ HEALTHY WEEKEND INDULGENCE

4 tomatoes
black pepper and basil (fresh if available) to
taste (optional)
4 eggs (organic free-range if possible)
2 slices gluten-free bread, toasted (if desired)

Place tomatoes under a broiler, and sprinkle with pepper and basil, if desired. Broil until soft and skins begin to split. While the tomatoes are broiling, fill a large frying pan with water and bring to a simmer. Poach the eggs in water for 3 minutes. Remove and set aside for another 30 seconds. Serve on toasted slices of bread.

✳ PORRIDGE WITH MIXED FRUIT

A serving of oats per day will help to stabilize blood sugar levels. If you're trying to give up smoking, then oatmeal could help, as it's believed to help fight cravings.

1 cup (100 g) apricots, halved
1 cup (100 g) raspberries
1 cup (100 g) pitted prunes, halved
2 ½ cups (225 g) oatmeal
filtered water

Place the fruits in a bowl, as you would a fruit salad, and combine. Place the oats in a saucepan, cover with plenty of water, and bring to a boil. Simmer for 5–10 minutes, stirring constantly, until thickened. Pour into a bowl and top with fruits.

LUNCHES

✳ STUFFED POTATO

4 small potatoes
1 small onion, finely chopped
1 clove garlic, finely chopped
1 tsp olive oil
1 tsp tomato puree
1 cup (110 g) cashew nuts, chopped
2 tbsp (30 g) gluten-free breadcrumbs
pinch mixed herbs
salt and pepper
1 organic free-range egg, beaten
extra oil for potato skins

Preheat the oven to 400ºF (200ºC). Boil the potatoes in their skins until cooked, about 20 minutes. Cut the potatoes in half, scoop out the flesh, and mash with a fork. Reserve the potato skins. Gently fry the onion and garlic in a little oil until cooked. Add the tomato puree and stir together. Mix this with the nuts, breadcrumbs, herbs, salt, and pepper, then stir in the mashed potato, adding the beaten egg. Brush the potato skins with oil, heap the mixture equally between the halves, and bake for 10–15 minutes. Can be served hot or cold. Makes 8 well-filled boats.

✳ SUN-DRIED TOMATO SOUP

Tomatoes, dried, fresh, or canned, are amongst the healthiest vegetables you can enjoy, and recent research has shown that they may help to reduce the risk of cancer. Tomatoes also contain lycopene, which can help fight against the negative effects of nicotine.

4 tbsp olive oil
9 cups (900 g) ripe plum tomatoes,
    halved lengthwise
2 cloves garlic, chopped
salt and freshly ground black pepper
3 ¾ cups (900 ml) vegetable stock
3 tbsp balsamic vinegar
½ cup (50 g) sun-dried tomatoes, shredded
4 diagonal slices of toasted
    gluten-free bread
mixed chopped herbs to garnish

Preheat the oven to 400ºF (200ºC). Place the oil in a large roasting pan and heat in the oven for a couple of minutes until almost smoking. Place the tomatoes in the roasting pan, skin-side down. Add garlic and seasoning. Bake for 40 minutes, until the tomatoes have dried and are browned. Remove tomatoes from the oven and put in a food processor or blender, along with any pan juices. Add the stock, balsamic vinegar, and sun-dried tomatoes and blend until smooth. Return the mixture to the pan and reheat for a few minutes. Garnish with the herbs and serve with the toast. Serves 4.

VEGETABLE AND BEAN SOUP

4 tbsp extra virgin olive oil (plus extra to drizzle)
1 large onion, finely chopped
2 cloves garlic, peeled and finely chopped
2 large zucchini, trimmed and grated
4 new potatoes, diced
1 large carrot, grated
6 ⅓ cups (1.5 liters) vegetable stock
2 x 2 ½ cups (250 g cans) flageolet beans

Heat oil in a large saucepan and fry the onion and garlic. Add the vegetables and continue stirring for 5 more minutes, then add the stock and beans. Bring to a boil and simmer for 20 minutes. Serve with a drizzle of oil. Serves 4.

STUFFED PEPPERS

Eating peppers can help increase your metabolic rate, so include them in your diet if you're watching your weight, especially after quitting smoking.

2 tbsp olive oil
1 red onion, chopped
1 clove garlic, chopped
1 cup (100 g) split red lentils
1 ¼ cups (300 ml) vegetable stock
freshly ground salt and black pepper
2 tomatoes, chopped
bunch fresh chives, snipped
4 red peppers, halved and deseeded

Preheat the oven to 400°F (220°C). Heat half the oil in a large frying pan and cook the onion and garlic for 5 minutes. Then add the lentils and the stock and bring to a boil, cover and simmer for 25 minutes, stirring occasionally until the lentils are tender and all the liquid is absorbed. Remove the pan from the heat and stir in the seasoning, tomatoes, and chives until well blended. Spoon into the peppers. Place the peppers on a baking sheet and drizzle with remaining olive oil. Bake for 30 minutes, until the peppers are tender. Serves 2–4.

DINNERS

✳ TOFU VEGETABLE SALAD

12 oz (375 g) firm tofu, drained

¾ cup (170 ml) bottled Italian vinaigrette
     salad dressing

2 medium zucchini

2 carrots

1 medium red pepper

5 cups (500 g) spinach, trimmed

2 ½ cups (250 g) cherry tomatoes

2 tbsp fresh chives, chopped

Cut tofu into ¾-inch (2-cm) cubes, and mix with the dressing in a bowl. (If you don't want to use store-bought salad dressing, just combine oil, lemon juice, and pepper with a little balsamic vinegar.) Cover and refrigerate for 10 minutes. Thinly slice the zucchini, carrots, and pepper. Combine the tofu mixture with vegetables and remaining ingredients in large bowl. Toss gently to mix. Serves 4.

✳ NOODLE SALAD WITH CHILI LEMONGRASS DRESSING

1 lb 2 oz (500 g) tofu or wild tuna

3 cups (300 g) hokkien noodles

2 tsp vegetable oil

5 cups (500 g) bok choy, chopped

5 cups (500 g) choy sum, chopped

1 bunch Chinese broccoli, chopped

1 cup bean sprouts

For the dressing:

2 tbsp chopped lemongrass

2 small fresh red chilies, deseeded and sliced

2 tbsp soy sauce

2 tbsp lime juice

1 tbsp grated fresh ginger

Preheat the oven to 340°F (170°C). Combine the tofu or tuna with one-third of the dressing in a bowl. Cover and refrigerate for 10 minutes. Place the undrained tofu or tuna on a smoking hot griddle and cook to your desired level.

Pour boiling water over noodles and let them stand for 5 minutes until tender, then drain. Heat the oil in a wok or large frying pan, quickly stir-fry bok choy, choy sum, and broccoli until the vegetables are just wilting. Combine the tofu or tuna with noodles, vegetables, bok choy, sprouts, and the remaining dressing in a bowl. Serves 4.

✳ BABY SPINACH AND POTATO SALAD

7 ¼ cups (720 g) tiny new potatoes, halved

8 tbsp (125 ml) olive oil

2 cups (200 g) baby spinach leaves

2 tbsp white wine vinegar

4 anchovy fillets in oil, drained

coarse black pepper to taste

Preheat oven to 430°F (220°C). Combine potatoes and 2 tablespoons of oil in a large baking dish. Bake uncovered for 25 minutes. Place the potatoes and spinach in a salad bowl. Blend the remaining ingredients and drizzle over salad. Add coarse black pepper to taste. Serves 4.

7-day total detox

So you've got the motivation. You've got the focus. You've even got the time. For the next seven days you're going to do nothing except eat healthily, exercise intensely, and concentrate on getting stronger and healthier than you've ever been in your life.

This 7-day cleansing and exercise plan is designed to eliminate toxins from your body, as well as energize your mind and body during this time. Of course, seven days isn't very long, so you should continue to apply the principles learned here for a healthier life.

Why you need this detox

☐ You need to lose weight

☐ Your exercise routine no longer exists

☐ You eat take-out meals more than four times a month

☐ You are reliant on coffee, cigarettes, and alcohol to get you through the week

☐ You can pinch more than an inch (of skin around your waist)

☐ Your skin is pallid, gray, and colorless

☐ You've had repetitive colds and illness for the past three months

☐ You have trouble sleeping, yet find it difficult to wake in the morning

☐ You find it difficult to muster enthusiasm for anything

Be aware that although you will definitely lose weight this week, most of it will be fluid. The aim of the 7-day detox is to kick-start your metabolism, so that over the coming weeks and months your body continues to level itself out, and you begin to lose excess weight. In addition, the exercise program will tone your body.

STEP ONE

Determine your Body Mass Index (BMI). You can work out your BMI with the following formula: BMI = weight in pounds divided by height in inches squared. Multiply the total by 703. For example: 63 inches X 63 inches = 3969 inches. BMI is 132 pounds divided by 3969, multiplied by 703 = 23.4

Your results:

Below 18.5	Underweight
18.5–24.9	Normal
25–29.9	Overweight
30+	Obese

Ideally, your BMI should be between 18.5 and 25. If it's higher or lower, then visit your health professional to ensure you are medically fit to begin this program.

STEP TWO

Measure yourself. This should include:

- hips
- thighs
- butt
- arms
- neck
- chest
- waist

These measurements will help you determine just how much your body changes during the seven days.

Write these down in a notepad so you can compare the difference after seven days (and as you continue with the health plan).

STEP THREE

Find a favorite pair of jeans/pants/dress that you can no longer fit into. If they're a size smaller than your current size, then in just a few weeks you'll have no problems zipping them up.

STEP FOUR

Get ready to move! Cutting down on alcohol, sugar, wheat, dairy, and fatty foods will only do so much: exercise is what really makes a difference to your overall health. Even just 30 minutes of exercise a day is enough to increase your metabolism and help raise your fitness levels. For the purpose of this week, we'll be ramping up your daily exercise quota to 40 minutes of intense cardiovascular work.

STEP FIVE

Get ready to eat! Unlike most diets, an intensive health overhaul doesn't require you to starve yourself. In fact, starving yourself actually slows down your metabolism and your body enters a "starvation mode." This means that it stores food as fat, as it is unsure of where its next meal is coming from. By feeding your body regularly, it will relax, and knowing that its next meal will be coming soon, it will happily burn food as fuel. Yo-yo dieting is the worst thing you can do to your body: constant yo-yo dieters actually accumulate weight around their hips. While the face and the chest are the first areas you lose weight, the hips and thighs are the first place you put it back on. So get ready to change your body shape and attitude towards food forever.

✳ YOUR FOOD NEEDS FOR THE WEEK

Buy
- Fish (tuna, prawns, salmon, mackerel)
- Vegetables (asparagus, spinach, carrots)
- Fruit (particularly lemons and grapefruit and superfoods, such as berries)
- Organic yogurt and dairy-free products
- Miso soup packets
- Fresh soup stock
- Herbal teas (licorice, dandelion, mint)
- Supplements (physilium husks, multivitamins, chromium)

Banish
- Caffeine (teas and coffee)
- Bread
- Dairy products
- Wheat products, such as pasta
- All pre-packaged foods, such as take-outs
- Sugary snacks and sugar

YOUR DAILY SCHEDULE

To ensure optimum results from these seven days, it's important to follow the schedule outlined below. It's not strict, but by eating and exercising at the same time every day, you'll help get your body and mind into a routine that you can continue in the future.

7:00 AM   Wake and early morning stretch

7:10 AM   Start each day with a cup of warm boiled water and lemon juice. Lemon juice will help you rebalance the alkaline/acid levels in your system and consequently help with any cravings you may encounter.

7:20 AM   Exercise program for that day (see pages 82–85 for day-by-day exercises)

8:20 AM   Body brush and shower (see page 96)

8:45 AM   Breakfast. Your first meal of the day is the most important one you'll have, yet many people skip it, even though research shows that people who skip breakfast are fatter than those who always make time for their cereal and coffee. In this plan you'll find easy, quick-to-prepare recipes that leave you no room for excuses.

9:30 AM   Rest and relaxation

10:30 AM   Snack (see page 81)

11:00 AM   Meditation (see page 116)

12:00 PM   Lunch

1:00 PM   Nap

2:00 PM   Journal writing (see page 59) or decluttering (see page 56)

3:00 PM   Snack

4:00 PM   Stretching (see page 82)

5:00 PM   Relaxation bath (see pages 46 and 96–97)

6:00 PM   Dinner preparation and meal

7:00 PM   Relaxation time

9:00 PM   Bed and lights out

Day one
BREAKFAST

✳ **ULTIMATE CLEANSER**

1 cup (100 g) broccoli
¾ cup (100 g) kale, chopped
1 cup (40 g) parsley
1 apple
2 sticks celery

Juice the ingredients and serve in a tall glass. Add pumpkin seeds, sunflower seeds or phsyllium husks if you like. This will help with any constipation you may suffer this week.

Take a milk thistle and chromium supplement.

LUNCH

✳ **LIMA BEAN, TOMATO, AND ARUGULA SALAD**
The lima beans in this salad will help to neutralize any acidity in your stomach, ideal for your first day of detoxing.

8 cups (800 g) plum tomatoes
6 cups (300 g) canned lima beans,
    rinsed and drained
1 salad (or Spanish) onion, chopped
1 ⅛ cups (120 g) arugula, trimmed,
    chopped roughly
2 tbsp slivered almonds, toasted

For the dressing:
2 cloves garlic, crushed
¾ cup (180 ml) olive oil
½ cup (125 ml) lemon juice
¼ cup (25 g) crushed parsley

3 tsp sweet paprika
1 tsp chili powder

Halve tomatoes lengthwise, remove seeds, slice thinly. To make the dressing, combine all the ingredients together in a bowl and mix well. Combine tomato, beans, onion, arugula, and dressing in a large bowl. Mix well. Serve topped with nuts. Serves 4.

DINNER

✳ **BAKED FILLET OF SOLE**
For optimum health and youthful looking skin you should eat fish at least three times a week as it is low in saturated fat and good for the brain.

4x 7 oz (200 g) fillet of sole
lemon juice
1 small onion, finely chopped
1 garlic clove, crushed
2 tbsp chopped parsley
salt and pepper
paprika
light soy sauce

Preheat oven to 375°C (190°C). Place fish in baking dish and brush with lemon juice. Sprinkle on onion, garlic, parsley, salt, pepper, and paprika. Soy sauce goes on last; use liberally. Bake for about 25 minutes. Serves 4.

Day Two
BREAKFAST

PORRIDGE WITH MIXED FRUIT
(see recipe page 56)

LUNCH

✳ BAKED FETA AND ROASTED TOMATO PASTA SALAD
Packed full of antioxidants, this salad is ideal if you're feeling a little under the weather, which may be the case on Day Two, as all those toxins start to leave your body.

3 cups (300 g) firm dairy-free soy feta
    cheese, chopped
8 tbsp (125 ml) olive oil
5 cups (500 g) cherry tomatoes
3 ¾ cups (375 g) penne pasta
    (gluten-free only)
⅛ cup (30 g) pine nuts, toasted
¼ cup (25 g) small fresh basil leaves,
    firmly packed
⅔ cup (60 g) pitted, sliced black olives

Preheat oven to 430°F (220°C). Place feta in a large piece of aluminum foil, bring the sides of the foil up around the cheese, and drizzle with 2 tablespoons of oil. Enclose cheese in foil. Place parcel at one end of shallow baking dish. Combine tomatoes with 1 tablespoon of the remaining oil in the same baking dish. Bake uncovered for about 15 minutes or until the tomatoes are soft. Meanwhile, cook pasta in large saucepan of boiling water, until just tender. Drain. Combine pasta, tomatoes, feta, and any pan juices in large bowl, stir through remaining oil, pine nuts, basil, and olives. Serves 4.

DINNER

✳ MUSSELS IN GINGER AND LEMONGRASS BROTH
Mussels are good for strengthening the liver, so are perfect for this week.

10 cups (1 kg) mussels, cleaned
3 cups (300 g) fish stock
2 tbsp shredded ginger
2 stalks lemongrass, finely chopped
2 tsp shredded lemon zest

Put the mussels in a sink of cold water and throw away any that stay open when tapped. Place stock, ginger, lemongrass, and lemon rind in a saucepan over heat. Bring the broth to a boil, then add the mussels and cook for 2–3 minutes or until the mussels have opened. Discard any mussels that don't open. Serve in deep bowls with the broth. Serves 4.

Day Three
BREAKFAST

✳ CLEAR SKIES
Cranberries contain digestive enzymes that help cleanse the lymphatic system. It is also excellent for helping level out your sugar levels.

½ grapefruit
1 kiwi fruit
large slice pineapple
⅔ cup (60 g) frozen cranberries
⅔ cup (60 g) frozen raspberries
lime wedge

Juice grapefruit, kiwi, and pineapple, then blend mixture with frozen berries. Add lime to taste.

LUNCH

✳ **SPINACH SALAD WITH WARM GARLIC DRESSING**

Spinach strengthens the blood and cleanses it of toxins—it's tasty raw or cooked. Add it to as many dishes as you can in the future.

2 ½ cups (250 g) baby spinach leaves
½ cup (50 g) semi-dried tomatoes
12 slices sourdough baguette
olive oil

Warm garlic dressing:
3 tbsp olive oil
3 cloves garlic, sliced
2 tbsp salted capers, rinsed
¼ cup (25 g) olives
2 tbsp lemon juice
2 tbsp thyme leaves
cracked black pepper

Place the spinach leaves and tomatoes on serving plates. Then put the baguette slices on a tray and drizzle with a little olive oil. Place under a hot broiler and toast for 1 minute or until lightly browned. To make the dressing, add the oil, garlic, capers, olives, lemon juice, thyme, and pepper to pan and cook for 1 minute or until heated through. Pour the warm dressing over the salad and top with the broiled baguette. Serves 4.

DINNER

✳ **LEMON AND PARSLEY FRIED FISH**

Lemons help to cleanse and improve blood circulation and also help calm the nerves. Served with fish, this is a great immune-boosting meal.

2 tbsp finely grated lemon rind
¼ tbsp chopped flat-leaf (Italian) parsley
cracked black pepper and sea salt
4 fillets of white fish
olive oil
lemon wedges, to serve
steamed greens, to serve

Combine the lemon rind, parsley, pepper, and salt in a bowl. Press the lemon and parsley mixture onto both sides of the fish. Heat a little olive oil in a large frying pan over high heat. Cook the fish for 1–2 minutes on each side or until cooked to your liking. Serve with lemon wedges and steamed greens. Serves 4.

Day Four
BREAKFAST

Bowl of organic muesli with added chopped fruits. Try adding apricots, prunes, apples, and kiwi fruit.

LUNCH

✳ PEA AND FAVA BEAN SOUP

Ideal for keeping your kidneys healthy. Peas are also a good source of vitamin C, as well as supplying the iron, carotenes, and B vitamins necessary for a healthy nervous system.

2 ¼ cups (225 g) frozen peas
2 ¼ cups (225 g) frozen broad beans
3 ¾ cups (900 ml) vegetable stock
salt and freshly ground black pepper
8 small slices gluten-free bread
1 clove garlic, sliced lengthwise
4 tbsp olive oil
plain organic yogurt
harissa paste

Place the peas, beans, and stock in a large saucepan and bring to a boil. Cover and simmer for 30 minutes, or until the beans are tender. Pour into a food processor or blender and blend until smooth. Pour back into the pan and heat through. Season. Place the bread slices on a broiler rack and rub the cut side of the clove of garlic over them. Drizzle over olive oil and toast under the broiler, turning once during cooking. To serve, pour the soup into bowls, place spoonfuls of yogurt on top, arrange two slices of bread on top, then spoon a little harissa over each. Serves 4.

DINNER

✳ CHICKEN AND BROCCOLI IN MUSHROOM SAUCE

If you're avoiding eating red meat, then increase your protein intake by eating chicken at least two to three times a week. Broccoli is one of the richest sources of iron, and is believed to help the body protect itself against cancer. It is also high in vitamins C and E and calcium.

3 tbsp vegetable oil
3 cups (300 g) fresh broccoli
4 tbsp soy margarine
2 ½ cups (250 g) fresh mushrooms, sliced
5 cups (500 g) chicken broth
⅓ cup (30 g) non-fat, non-dairy organic milk or
    almond, oat, or rice milk
⅔ cups (65 g) rice flour
½ green onion, sliced
nutmeg
1 lb 2 oz (500 g) cooked chicken
2 tbsp finely chopped parsley

Preheat oven to 375°F (190°C). Add vegetable oil to bottom of baking dish; set aside. Steam broccoli until tender. Drain and blot dry on paper towels; set aside. In a medium non-stick skillet over medium heat, melt 1 tablespoon soy margarine. Add sliced mushrooms, cover, and cook 7–9 minutes, or until mushrooms have released all their juices. Uncover and increase setting to high. Allow liquid to evaporate. Set aside. In a small bowl, combine chicken broth and non-fat, non-dairy organic milk or almond, oat, or rice milk. Set aside. In a medium saucepan, melt 3 tablespoons soy margarine over medium-high heat. Stir in flour and cook 1 minute. Add chicken broth mixture and stir with wire whisk. Bring to a boil, then add onion and nutmeg. Add cooked mushrooms and set aside. Lay broccoli on bottom of prepared pan. Evenly distribute chicken over broccoli. Pour mushroom sauce over all. Sprinkle parsley on top. Bake for 25 minutes. Serves 6.

Day Five
BREAKFAST

✳ **SPEED IT UP**

1 cup (250 ml) apple juice
handful blueberries
handful raspberries
1 banana
1 kiwi fruit
½ cup (50 g) pumpkin seeds
½ cup (50 g) sunflower seeds

Put all ingredients into a blender. Blend at a high speed until the mixture is smooth. Add ice if desired.

LUNCH

✳ **MILLET MEDLEY**

Avocados are thought to be a "complete" food, as they are highly nutritious, particularly in vitamin E, an important vitamin for healthy skin, hair, and nails.

2¼ cups (225 g) millet
1 red onion, diced
2 avocados, peeled, stoned, diced
1 red pepper, diced
8 cherry tomatoes, quartered
¾ cup (75 g) mushrooms, quartered
4 tbsp pumpkin seeds and sunflower seeds

For the dressing:
6 tbsp olive oil
2 tbsp cider vinegar
4 tbsp chopped fresh mixed herbs
1 tbsp tahini paste
juice of 1 lemon
sea salt and ground black pepper

Place the millet in a large bowl and pour over just enough boiling water to cover. Leave it to stand for 45 minutes until the liquid is absorbed and the millet is cool. Using a fork, break into fine grains. Stir the onion, avocado, pepper, tomatoes, and mushrooms into the millet. (Ideally, the vegetables should be raw for this dish, but you can lightly steam them if you prefer.) Whisk together the dressing ingredients and toss through the salad, along with the seeds.
Serves 4.

DINNER

✳ VEGETABLE AND PRAWN SKEWERS

This meal is packed full of health-giving nutrients and antioxidants. Prawns are full of skin-boosting omega-3s and the pineapple is also believed to help speed up your metabolic rate.

2½ cups (250 g) fresh prawns
2 peppers, cored, deseeded, and cut into
    large chunks
4 large onions, sliced and cut into quarters
5 cups (500 g) mushrooms, peeled and
    cut into quarters
5 cups (500 g) pineapple chunks
    (can be canned variety)
2½ cups (250 g) zucchini, cut into thick slices
honey or olive oil (optional)

Lightly broil or fry the prawns to ensure they're evenly cooked through. Pre-heat the broiler. While this is warming up, thread all ingredients onto skewers, alternating them. Brush with honey or olive oil if desired. Place on a baking tray and broil for 4–5 minutes, turning as cooked. Garnish with salad. Serves 4.

Day Six
BREAKFAST

✳ WEEKEND TREATS

Try to include protein in all of your meals. Your body will burn up more calories digesting protein, plus it will help sustain your energy.

2 organic free-range eggs
½ cup (150 ml) soy milk
1 slice wild smoked salmon

1 slice toasted gluten-free bread
chives
black pepper

Scramble the eggs, adding the milk (as much or as little according to your taste). Keep the heat low as you don't want the eggs too rubbery. Place the smoked salmon on the toast, and serve the eggs on top when ready. Add chives and black pepper to taste.

LUNCH

✳ LIME, TOMATO, AND SCALLOP SALAD

Limes are high in vitamin C, and, served with scallops, this salad provides all the nutrients needed as you continue your detox.

2 ½ cups (250 g) rice noodles
5 cups (500 g) scallops
1 tbsp sweet chili sauce
1 tbsp lime juice
2 ½ cups (250 g) trimmed, chopped
    asparagus
3 ⅓ cups (330 g) cherry tomatoes, halved
¼ cup (25 g) slivered almonds, toasted

For the dressing:
½ cup (125 ml) peanut oil
2 tbsp chopped fresh cilantro
1 tbsp chopped fresh mint leaves
2 small fresh red chilies, deseeded, quartered
¼ cup (60 ml) lime juice

Place noodles in large heatproof bowl, cover with boiling water and leave for a couple of minutes until just tender, drain. Rinse under cold water and drain. Combine all dressing ingredients and set aside. Broil the scallops in batches. Combine chili sauce and lime juice and brush the scallops as they cook. Steam asparagus until just tender, rinse under cold water, then drain. Gently toss noodles, scallops, and asparagus in a large bowl with the tomatoes and the dressing. Sprinkle with almonds. Serves 4.

DINNER

✳ MARINATED CHICKEN WITH PRUNE SALSA

Eating prunes is a great way to fulfil your daily iron intake, which is necessary to support your fitness program. They're also ideal for your digestive system—add them to your juice and cereals too, or keep them on hand for snacks.

1 tbsp olive oil
1 tbsp tomato paste
1 tbsp honey
1 tbsp soy sauce
4 skinless chicken breasts

Salsa:
1½ cups (150 g) prunes
1 raw chili, finely chopped
1 medium tomato, deseeded and chopped
1 tbsp of olive oil
Juice of ½ lime
1 tbsp each of cilantro and mint

To make the salsa, put the prunes in a pan of water and bring to a boil, then take off the heat and allow to soak for about an hour. Combine the chili, tomato, oil, and lime together. When the prunes are ready, chop roughly, removing and discarding the stones, then add to the salsa, and chill.

Mix olive oil, tomato paste, honey, and soy sauce together and spread over the chicken breasts, leave for about 1 hour to marinate, turning the breasts over halfway through to allow the marinade to cover the chicken completely. The chicken can be cooked by a variety of methods, baking in the oven for about 20–25 minutes at 425ºF (220ºC), broiling, dry frying in a heavy broiler pan, or grilling. Before serving add the mint and cilantro to the salsa. Serves 4.

Day Seven
BREAKFAST

✳ SMOKED HADDOCK KEDGEREE WITH BROILED TOMATOES

This is a typical English dish, much favored as a hearty breakfast as it's warm and hearty and can help undo the effects of a hangover. Haddock is an excellent detox food as it contains protein, iodine and B vitamins. Teamed with the anti-cancer properties of tomatoes, this is an ideal breakfast for those who want a heartier meal.

1½ cups (150 g) smoked haddock fillet
1 free-range egg (organic if possible)
1 cup (100 g) brown basmati rice
2 large tomatoes
2 tsp freshly chopped parsley
paprika

Place the fish in a small pan containing about ¼ cup (50 ml) water. Cover with a lid and steam for 7–8 minutes. Hard boil the egg, then peel and chop it. Place 1 cup (250 ml) water in a pan and bring to a boil. Add the rice, stir, and cover with a lid. Reduce the heat and leave to cook for about 20–25 minutes. The rice should be cooked and the water absorbed. Cut the tomatoes in half and broil for 5–6 minutes. Stir the haddock, egg, and parsley into the rice. This will make the rice fluffy. Serve with the tomatoes and add paprika to taste. Serves 2.

SNACKS FOR MORNING AND AFTERNOON

✳ ENERGY JUICE

1 apple
1 pear
1 banana
nuts and seeds (optional)
1 tbsp organic dairy-free yogurt

Juice the apple and pear, and pour liquid into a blender. Add the banana—plus nuts and seeds, if desired—and yogurt. Blend until smooth. Add ice if required and drink immediately.

✳ FRESH FRUIT WITH MAPLE-VANILLA YOGURT DIP

Increase your daily intake of fresh fruit with this tasty and nutritious yogurt dip. You can use any type of yogurt, as long as it's low-fat.

2⅛ cups (500 ml) vanilla low-fat organic yogurt
1⅓ cups (125 g) maple syrup
1 apple
1 pear
juice of 1 lemon

1 tbsp crushed pistachio nuts
5 cups (500 g) grapes

Combine the yogurt and maple syrup, and place in the refrigerator to chill. Core and slice the apple and pear. Sprinkle with lemon juice to prevent discoloration. Place the yogurt in a bowl in the center of a large platter and drizzle the yogurt with a few extra drops of maple syrup, then sprinkle with the pistachio nuts. Arrange the apples, pears, and grapes on the platter. Serves 8.

✳ TASTY TUNA SNACK

This easy-to-make snack will fill you up, so you'll be less likely to reach for the cookie jar!

juice of ½ lemon
½ can light tuna (in water)
lettuce
2 small tomatoes, chopped
1 celery stick, chopped finely
½ carrot, chopped
black pepper
1 slice gluten-free bread

Pour half the lemon juice over the tuna. Place lettuce on a plate. Combine tuna, tomatoes, celery, and carrot in a small bowl, then place on top of the lettuce. Serve with a little more lemon juice, pepper to taste, and a slice of gluten-free bread.

Other snack ideas: handful of dried fruit (especially apricots, figs, and prunes), nuts (although no more than a handful, as they are high in calories), hummus on gluten-free crackers, and seeds.

Exercise

Now you've learned what to eat, it's time to think about how to keep that newly healthy body of yours in peak condition through the practice of a series of disciplines, some of which you will never have tried before (rock climbing) and others with which you will be more familiar (swimming). Once you've tried this exciting program as part of your 7-day detox plan you will positively relish the idea of exercise!

Day One
WEIGHT TRAINING

This ancient workout is hard—really, really hard. When I first started training with kettlebells I couldn't even walk up the stairs afterwards. But the results are well worth it. Kettlebells are those old-fashioned hand weights you used to see strongmen lifting—they've been repackaged as the full body workout. Just 10 minutes of exercising with kettlebells is equivalent to 45 minutes running on a treadmill. They're hard work, but well worth it. You will need to buy kettlebells—and they range in weight from 11 lbs (5 kg) upward. It is best to start with the lightest weights and work your way up toward heavier ones. If you can't get ahold of any, you could use a filled water bottle or an ordinary hand weight.

After a warm-up jog of 5 minutes, you're ready to do a kettlebell workout. Try the following workout during your 7-day detox.

Front squat

Hold the weight to your chest and lower your body into a squat. Hold, then, using your thighs as propellers, lift yourself back into a standing position. Repeat three sets of ten, and run for 100 yards (90 meters) between each set.

The swing

Standing with your feet apart, hold the weight between your legs. Swing it back and forth until you have momentum going. Swing the weight backwards and forwards, "snapping" the weight when it's at its highest point in front of you.

Repeat for three sets of ten, and run 100 yards (90 meters) between each set.

The lift

Holding the weight by the handle lift it above your head, making sure that your arm is vertical from your shoulder and behind your ears. Repeat for three sets of ten. Run 100 yards (90 meters) between each set.

STRETCHING

Stretching is just as important as the rest of your exercise program, as it helps to cool down your body and prevent injury. Try to include stretching in your exercise plan everyday.

Standing facing a wall, bend one leg behind you and grasp your ankle, pulling it towards your buttocks. Pull until you feel a tightening in your thigh. Hold for the count of ten. Release and repeat on the other leg.

Place your left arm across your body, grasping your upper arm with the opposite one. Pull the arm tightly to your chest until you feel the stretch in your upper arm and shoulder.

Stand with your feet shoulder-width apart and your arms loosely by your sides. Place your tongue gently against the roof of your mouth and bend your head down, toward your chest. Hold, then slowly tip your head backward until you're looking upward. Repeat five times, taking care to move your head slowly and carefully.

Day Two
SWIMMING

Diving into a cool pool is a wonderful way to clear your mind. But this workout is designed to speed up your heart rate and tone your arms and thighs.

For a productive workout, swim one lap at your usual rate (over arm if possible) then one lap as fast as you possibly can. By alternating your speeds you'll work your body harder and get better results, faster. Start with as many laps as you can manage, keeping in mind that over the coming weeks as you continue with this fitness plan, you'll increase your workout by two laps each week. If you can't swim, or dislike swimming, then join an aqua aerobic class instead. This workout is light on your joints and whatever your weight, you'll feel as light as a feather.

Day Three
LONG WALK

Walking is the best exercise around. It's free, it's easy, almost everyone can do it, and you can do it anywhere, as long as you have a pathway in front of you. Walking has many benefits: it's easy on the joints, lowers the chances of heart disease and diabetes, and is believed to be an effective antidepressant. It tones the hips, buttocks, and waist and, done three times a week, is a great way to boost your fitness levels.

Make sure you have the appropriate footwear (visit a specialist sports store for your needs) and wear layers of clothing that you can peel off as you warm up (and put back on as you cool down after). Swing your arms back and forward in time with your step—this helps boost the cardiovascular effect. Keep your shoulders and head relaxed and step forward firmly and evenly.

Walk for 1 hour at a comfortable pace—you shouldn't be able to hold a conversation, but neither should you be gasping for breath.

Cool down and make sure you stay warm. Follow with stretches.

Day Four
HOT YOGA, SUCH AS BIKRAM YOGA

Hot Yoga is practiced in a room heated to 95–100°F (35–38°C). The high room temperature allows for a loosening of tight muscles and profuse sweating, which is believed to be cleansing.

WALK

An afternoon walk will help clear the cobwebs and stretch those sore, tired muscles. It doesn't need to be longer than 20 minutes—why not walk to a newspaper stand and pick up a copy of your favorite magazine? Then you can relax when you get home.

Day Five
BOXING

Boxing has become an extremely popular sport and is no longer just the domain of men. More and more women are discovering the powerful rush gained from a bout in the ring. Boxing tones your entire body, as well as helping focus your mind. It's especially good if you're stressed. Make sure that you box in a supervised environment. Boxing can cause injuries, not only to yourself, but to others.

Push forward with your forearm, not your shoulder, otherwise you can jar the joint. Your focus should be on the movement of delivering a blow, not the power of it. This way you'll experience a full upper body workout.

Attend a class today and find out whether you've discovered a new passion.

Day Six
ROCK CLIMBING

Another exercise that will stretch your body and mind. Rock climbing has increased in popularity over the years—both indoor and outdoor courses are available in even the most urban areas. It's a total body workout and burns almost 1000 calories an hour, as well as toning your arms, shoulders, back, thighs, and calves. Women are usually very adept at picking up the tricks of rock climbing, because our upper bodies are weaker than our male counterparts, and so we're used to using our legs as our main source of strength. You won't be allowed on a rock climbing wall without first undergoing instruction, so have this booked before you begin your detox week. Believe us though, after the first time you reach the top of the wall, you'll be ready to come back for more.

Day Seven
RUN

You've had a busy week, and you probably feel like a rest. Well, there's no rest for the wicked! Put on those running shoes and set off for your local park. Running outside is preferable to a running machine for a number of reasons. The first being the mechanics. Running on land you are propelling yourself forward over ground whereas on a treadmill the ground moves under you. Often people become efficient at running on a treadmill by "hanging" or "floating" and not actually moving forward as should happen when you run on the ground. In addition you will just feel better being outside with the fresh air, sunlight, and vitamin D compared with the stuffy air-conditioned atmosphere you get in the gym.

During your run, try repeating a sequence of 60 seconds of sprinting followed by 2 minutes of jogging. This alternative speed helps to burn fat quicker, as well as give your body a more vigorous workout. If you find it tiring, then just try it for 5–10 minutes and work your way up by increasing your workout in 2 minute increments every day.

Your footwear is just as important as your workout. The correct footwear can enhance your workout, while the incorrect pair of shoes can actually hinder it. For the best footwear, visit a sporting goods store to discuss your needs. Your shoes should fit snugly, but not too tight. Remember that your feet will swell during a workout as they get warmer. And make sure to try the shoes on with the same sort of socks you train in. Your running shoes should feel light—not heavy or cumbersome.

detox
body treatments

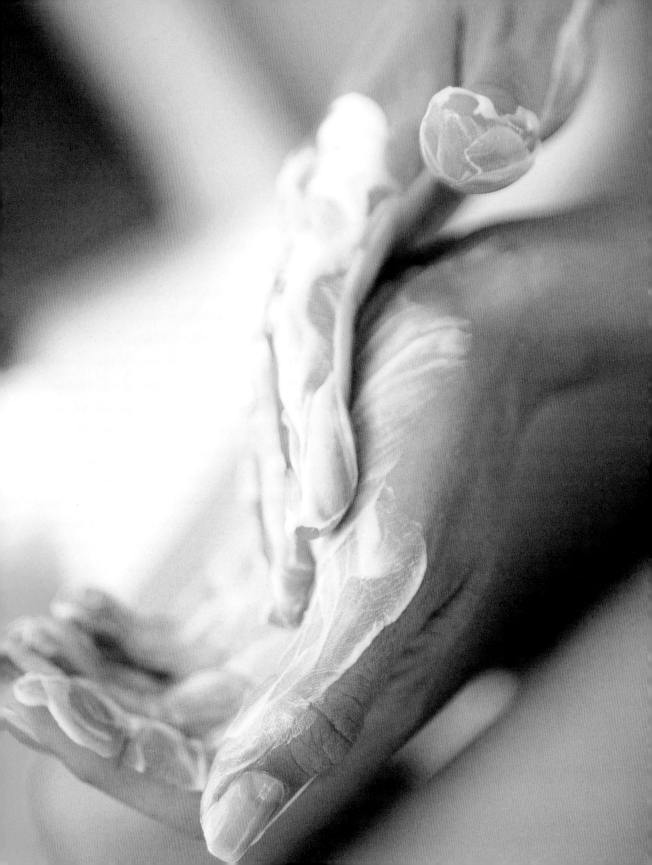

Beauty boosting plans

Skin is your largest organ (both by weight and surface area) and usually the first place that illnesses or symptoms show. For example, if your hair is dry and splitting, it usually means that you need more essential fatty acids and oils in your diet (eating salmon is an excellent means of obtaining these). If your nails are flaking, you probably haven't been taking in enough calcium. And if your skin is blotchy and spotty then it's possible that your liver isn't dealing with toxins correctly. Your skin offers very useful insight into the state of your health.

Why you need this detox

1. Is your forehead lined?

This may indicate that your urinary tract or kidneys are sluggish. Drinking at least 4 pints (2 liters) of water per day will help.

2. Are your eyes slightly cloudy or red?

If it's not because of lack of sleep or a hangover, then your liver could be suffering. Take milk thistle and cut down on your alcohol and caffeine intake.

3. Has your nose reddened or does it have broken capillaries?

Your circulatory system may be lagging. Try including vitamin B foods, such as bananas, into your diet, get more exercise, and drink more water (at least 3 pints (1.5 liters) per day).

4. Do you have spots along your jaw line?

These could be caused by stress and/or a problematic digestive tract. Concentrate on lowering your stress levels, and drink warm water with lemon juice first thing every morning.

5. Do you have spots on your chin?

This could be caused by hormonal issues or problems with your small intestines. Take agnus castus, and avoid chocolate around your menstrual due date.

6. Do you have spots on your back or chest?

Again your liver may be the culprit. Milk thistle helps to regenerate your liver and its ability to detoxify. Drinking hot water in the morning with lemon juice also helps.

7. Is your complexion dull and gray?

You may be dehydrated or suffering from an overload of toxins. Drink at least 4 pints (2 liters) of bottled or filtered water a day. Avoid bread, sugars, and fried food for at least ten days.

How the skin works

Your skin is made up of several layers. The bottom layer, the dermis, is composed of connective tissue, blood vessels, nerve ending hair follicles, and sweat and oil glands; and the top layer, the epidermis, which is visible to the naked eye, renews itself every 15–30 days.

Your skin retains less moisture as you age. Just compare the skin of a 15 year old to that of a 50 year old—the main difference is the existence of wrinkles and suppleness of the epidermis in the older skin. There's not much you can do about holding back the hands of time forever, but whatever your age, you can certainly have clear glowing skin at all times. How? It's all down to your diet, lifestyle, and yes, even your mental attitude.

Lifestyle and your skin

The phrase "you are what you eat" isn't just about your butt and your jeans size. It also refers to your appearance and how it reflects your lifestyle. For instance, have a couple of late nights out in a row, and the next day those glasses of wine and midnight pizza will reappear in the form of puffy eyes and pale, blotchy skin. A few early nights in though, and you'll be rewarded with clear, glowing eyes and skin, and comments from friends about how "rested" you look.

This is because our skin feeds off the food and moisture we put into our mouths. As our skin is

constantly renewing itself and our hair and nails constantly growing, we need the nutrients from food to fuel this activity. The words "feed your face" are your new mantra!

Feeding your face: foods to enjoy

Certain foods are particularly beneficial as beauty boosters. Try some of the following suggestions.

POMEGRANATE

For: *clear skin, may help against aging*
Pomegranates contain free radicals, which fight against external factors (such as pollution, cigarette smoke, and fats) that may accelerate signs of aging. The juice of a pomegranate is one of nature's most powerful antioxidants.
Recommended dosage: *one per day or 8.5 fl oz (250 ml) of pomegranate juice is ideal for smooth, youthful-looking skin*

BLUEBERRIES

For: *antiaging, preventing dry skin, gum disease, bloodshot eyes*
Hailed as a "superfood," these gorgeously-colored berries are not only a low-calorie snack, but can also help you look and feel younger. Blueberries contain flavonoids, which help to neutralize free radicals, and strengthen the collagen in the walls of the blood vessels in the eyes. They're also rich in vitamin C, which helps to keep the skin supplied with oxygen and nutrients. If you smoke, then blueberries will help counteract the harmful aging affects of nicotine (although not as well as giving up will!).
Recommended dosage: *a handful of blueberries added to a smoothie or with porridge*
Also eat: *all berries, such as goji, acai, strawberries, raspberries, and apricots*

PEPPERS

For: *dry, flaking nails*

Peppers have a high water content—one large pepper supplies the body with the equivalent of a glass of water, so they are particularly useful for keeping the skin and nails hydrated. Nails are 16 percent water and when the levels fall below this they become prone to brittleness, breakage and peeling. Peppers are also packed full of vitamin C, which helps boost the immune system and fight fungal infections.

Also eat: *herrings, garlic, and black-eyed peas*

PRAWNS

For: *soft, dewy skin*

Prawns are ideal if your skin has lost some of its luster and softness. They contain copper, vital for creating collagen and springy elastin, which form the deeper layers of the skin. Copper also helps to absorb ultraviolet rays and creates an even, natural skin color.

Also eat: *seaweed, strawberries, wholewheat bread*

CHAMOMILE

For: *dark eye circles*

Dark circles around the eyes can be caused by a sluggish liver or kidneys, so drinking herbal tea, such as camomile, can help kick-start these organs. Chamomile is also a natural antiseptic, and can help reduce redness of the eye and blocked tear ducts. If you're suffering from a lack of sleep, try drinking camomile tea before going to bed. The balerianic acid in the leaves of the camomile plant can help you relax. A good night's sleep is beauty's restorer, reducing the appearance of dark circles and also reducing the appearance of tiredness and facial tension. These can add years, so try and get a minimum of 8 hours at least once a week.

Also eat/drink: *warm water with lemon, prunes, yellow peppers*

AVOCADO

For: *dry skin*

Avocado really is the skin-saver of the food world. You can use avocados externally to moisturize dry, damaged skin, or eat them for numerous complexion benefits. Avocados contain around 1 oz (28 g) of fat, which helps to plump out skin cells, and provides the nourishment needed to prevent dryness and wrinkles. The monounsaturated oils can also help to reduce inflamed skin conditions, such as eczema, acne, or psoriasis. For dietary reasons, choose Florida-grown avocados, which contain half the fat, and two-thirds the calories of California-grown ones.

Also eat: *salmon, nuts, seeds, papaya*

PUMPKIN SEEDS

For: *soft, shiny hair*

Pumpkin seeds are not just a tasty snack; they're also a great way to add some shine to your hair. They contain a large amount of iron, which helps supply oxygen to the hair roots, and can help prevent hair loss. Iron will also encourage hair to grow much faster. The protein in pumpkin seeds also helps build keratin, the protective coating of hair that makes it appear shiny. And if you're growing your hair but despair of your split ends, then the zinc helps to strengthen the hair follicle.

Also eat: *flax seeds, mackerel, tuna*

WALNUTS

For: *rich hair color*

If your hair color is fading, then try adding some walnuts to your diet. Walnuts contain copper, which is needed by the body to produce melanin pigments. Melanin gives hair its color, and it also helps thicken and add shine to hair. Eating walnuts may also help reverse the graying of hair. Including walnuts in your diet can also increase blood flow to the head and scalp, which means that your hair will grow faster.
Also eat: *legumes, seafood*

OATS

For: *white spots on nails*

This may indicate that you are lacking in vitamin E. Try adding some oats to your diet, to make sure you get sufficient levels. Vitamin E helps to keep nails healthy and strong. Oats also contain iron; a deficiency can lead to thin, brittle nails, with a concave shape.
Also eat: *pine nuts, sesame seeds, cashew nuts*

SCALLOPS

For: *oily skin*

Scallops are high in protein, yet very low in fat. They contain significant amounts of omega-3 fat, which helps prevent heart disease and counteracts inflammation. They are also good sources of minerals including the antioxidants selenium and zinc. If you suffer from excessively dry or oily skin, or you break out in spots on a regular basis, you could be deficient in zinc, which is vital for skin repair and renewal.
Also try: *prawns, anchovies, mussels*

YOGURT

For: *dry, cracked lips*

If you suffer from sore lips, particularly in the colder months, it may indicate a lack of riboflavin, or vitamin B2. This deficiency can cause an inflammation of cells in the lips, causing swelling and cracks. Prolonged periods of constipation can lead to spots around the mouth. Eating a bowl of natural unsweetened organic yogurt every day can help maintain a healthy gut and prevent constipation.
Also eat: *chicken, cranberries*

KIWI FRUIT

For: *cellulite*

The "orange peel" appearance affects around 95 percent of women. Eating kiwi fruit, which is extremely high in vitamin C, not only helps you achieve your five-a-day fruit and vegetable goal, but eating just one means you've achieved more than your recommended daily intake of vitamin C. This vitamin is required to help strengthen capillary walls, which, when ruptured, can cause skin bruising and tiny thread veins. Strong capillary walls also ensure a good supply of oxygen and nutrients can reach the skin, helping it appear plumper and smoother and more elastic.
Also try: *celery, berries, papaya*

Foods to avoid

If you really want to look your best, then taking a firm hand to your diet will pay dividends to your appearance. Avoid all processed and fast-foods, as they tend to be loaded with salt, sodium, monosodiumglutamate, sugars, and fats, none of which are needed by your skin (or the rest of your body for that matter). Sugar, in particular, is believed to be more aging than smoking, so if you want to look as young as possible, for as long as possible, cut out all sugary snacks.

Your beauty boosting eating plan

This eating plan can (and should) be accommodated as much as possible into your everyday life. Sure, there's room for a glass of wine or two, and yes, you can indulge in (dark) chocolate every couple of days too. Remember, it's how you live most of the time that counts—the occasional indulgence in your favorite treat won't hurt you or your skin.

BEFORE YOU EAT

A glass of warm water and lemon juice will do wonders not only for your liver, but also your skin. Use a fresh lemon and add to warm, boiled water and drink before eating every day.

BREAKFAST

✳ BANANA SMOOTHIE

Good for: energy, lackluster skin and tired eyes
(see recipe on page 38)

PORRIDGE WITH MIXED FRUIT

(see recipe on page 56)

LUNCH

✳ COUSCOUS MEDLEY

Good for: hair, skin, and nails

2¼ cups (225 g) couscous
2¼ cups (225 g) smoked streaky bacon
1 red onion, diced
2 avocados, peeled, stoned, diced
4 tbsp pumpkin seeds

For the dressing:
6 tbsp olive oil
2 tbsp cider vinegar
4 tbsp chopped fresh mixed herbs
1 tbsp tahini paste
juice of 1 lemon
sea salt and ground black pepper

Place the couscous in a large bowl and pour over just enough boiling water to cover. Leave to stand for 45 minutes until liquid is absorbed and couscous is cool. Using a fork, break into fine grains. Broil the bacon for 10 minutes, turning occasionally, until golden. Remove from heat and snip into strips. Stir the onion and avocado into the couscous. Whisk together the dressing ingredients and toss through the salad. Divide the couscous between serving plates. Scatter over the bacon and pumpkin seeds. Serves 4.

DINNER

✳ SALMON STEAKS WITH SESAME SEED CRUSTS

Good for: helps hair and nails grow stronger. Regular intakes of salmon are also believed to help alleviate the signs of aging.

4 salmon steaks
juice and grated zest of 1 lime
salt and freshly ground black pepper
3 tbsp sesame seeds
2 tbsp flat leaf parsley, chopped
1 sliced white rice cake, made into crumbs
2 tbsp sunflower seeds
1 red chili, deseeded and finely chopped
3 tbsp olive oil

Place the salmon steaks in a shallow dish. Pour over the lime juice and zest, and season. Turn to coat and leave to marinate for 10 minutes. Mix together the sesame seeds, parsley, crumbs, sunflower seeds, and chili in a large bowl. Remove the salmon from the lime juice and dip into the sesame seed mixture, coating well. Heat the oil in a large frying pan and cook the salmon for 3–4 minutes on each side until golden. Remove from the heat and serve on a bed of salad leaves. Serves 4.

SNACKS

Fruit, such as prunes, apricots, and apples are ideal. Alternatively you could snack on seeds such as pumpkin, sunflower, or hemp, all of which contain essential fatty acids that help smooth your skin and provide it with moisture.

LIQUIDS

Drink at least 3 pints (1.5 liters) of water every day. Not only is it nature's best beauty treatment, but it's also free. Water is needed for healthy, youthful-looking skin, as it plumps up the epidermis, making it look smooth and dewy. Drinking around 3 pints (1.5 liters) of water each day will also help to keep your liver and kidneys cleansed, as it assists in flushing out toxins (see page 18 for more information on the liver). You don't have to spend a fortune on bottled water, just attach a filter to your tap or invest in a filter pitcher. Room temperature water is best. If you find the taste of water boring, then add a squeeze of fresh lemon or lime.

Teas such as green, white, or specialist blends such as detox teas, are a great way to increase your liquid intake as well as boost your antioxidant levels. Just make sure that the green tea is decaffeinated.

To drink or not to drink?

Alcohol that is. Numerous studies have highlighted the aging effects of overdoing the drinking, yet there is nothing better than a glass of red wine on a cold winter's night. So how can you enjoy a drink without ending up with a red bulbous nose and saggy cheeks? Like everything, drinking wine in moderation is highly unlikely to damage your skin, and in fact, some research shows that one or two glasses of red wine a day is recommended for preventing some cancers, slowing the aging process, and lowering stress levels. Try to abstain from opening a bottle from Sunday night to Thursday night, so that you're only drinking two to three nights a week. It might be difficult at first (and you may even go completely overboard on the Friday night, thus undoing all your good work), but the longer you practice these good habits, the less likely it will be that you'll overindulge and suffer the consequences the following day (both internally and externally).

Facial massage

Ideally, getting a facial once a month should be part of your life, but you can also help yourself to relax your frown lines and stimulate circulation for a healthy glow. Try to spend time on your skin at least once a week. Be careful not to tug or pull at it though, and always work upwards—against gravity.

STEP ONE

Place your hands on either side of your cheeks, with your fingertips resting lightly underneath your eyes. Imaging you are playing the piano and gently tap the notes out underneath your eyes. This will help to eliminate any dark puffy eye bags.

STEP TWO

Repeat the process on an area just below. Work your way around your face, across the cheeks, down to the chin, across the forehead and finish at the temples by pressing firmly.

STEP THREE

Finish the face massage by cupping your hands over your closed eyes and breathing deeply.

STEP FOUR

Exhale. When ready, move your hands and slowly open your eyes.

Treatments at home

Although I'm a big fan of day spas and treating yourself to a massage, sometimes budgets just won't allow it. But there's no need to miss out. A spa treatment at home is just as viable (and effective). Try some of these favorites.

Dry skin brushing

Increase your circulation and improve the texture of your skin with some morning skin brushing. Daily skin brushing using a loofah or long-handed natural bristle brush will eliminate dead cells and also unblock the pores, as well as kick-starting the lymph system. This is an ideal treatment for circulation and beating cellulite, so it should be performed daily. It takes hardly any time and you'll notice the difference within a week.

HOW TO SKIN BRUSH

Starting from the fet upwards, brush the skin in long sweeps all the way up your body toward your heart and lymph glands to get the blood pumping, and crank up the system.

Not only will you see tiny dead skin cells float away but it will also get the circulation going. This is also a great way of combating cellulite. Your skin will redden but don't be alarmed. If you take just a few minutes everyday before you bath or shower you will see the benefits.

Detoxifying baths

Baths are wonderfully healing, and it is easy to make your own detox baths. Hot water draws toxins to the skin's surface, and as the water cools it pulls toxins from the skin.

DETOX BATH

Minerals and salts leave your skin cleansed and soft, plus the magnesium in Epsom salts helps to relax sore and tired muscles.

1 cup (100 g) Epsom salts
5 drops lavender essential oil

Pour the Epsom salts into the bath as it is filling. Add the lavender a few minutes before you hop in.

Caution: Do not take hot baths and salt baths (including Epsom salt baths) if you have heart trouble, high blood pressure, or are diabetic.

Body Treatments

From top to toe—a fantastic selection of treatments for your body.

DETOX FOOT TREATMENT

Treating the whole foot can have a relaxing, balancing, detoxing, and healing effect on the whole body—reflex areas in the feet and hands correspond to certain parts of the body.

You can give yourself a reflexology treatment—or bribe your partner into massaging your feet—to help you make the most of your detox. The following are ideal pressure points if you want to speed up the detoxification process.

- Big toes—good if you're suffering from a headache
- Ball of foot—relates to your neck and shoulders; relieves tension
- Arch of foot—relates to liver, bowel, and kidney. This may be tender if you've been burning the candle at both ends or just begun a detox. Press gently, otherwise you may over-stimulate the bowel.
- Top of foot—calms the mind

ALL OVER BODY PAMPER

Using essential oils can help hydrate extremely dry skin and return it to its natural moisture level.

10 drops lavender
10 drops Roman chamomile
10 drops neroli
10 drops rosemary
10 drops carrot seed
⅔ cup (60 g) almond, olive, or sesame oil

Apply the oil once a day after bathing or showering, while your skin is still damp. This helps your body retain moisture from bathing.

COCOA BUTTER CREAM

Ideal for pregnant women, but also anyone who suffers from stretch marks. Use after showering to maintain moisture.

1 ¼ cups (125 g) cocoa butter
1 tsp almond oil
1 tsp vitamin E oil

Place all the ingredients in an ovenproof glass container and gently heat in the microwave, or over a pan of boiling water, until the cocoa butter is melted and the oils are well mixed. Pour into a clean container and allow the cream to cool completely. You may need to stir the cream one more time after it has cooled. Store in a container in a cool, dry place.

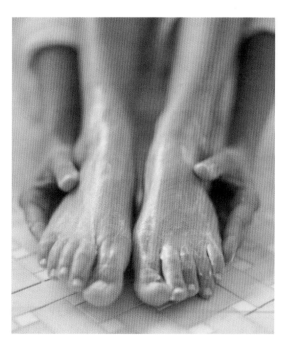

THIRSTY SKIN MOISTURIZER

Avocado is not just a tasty fruit, it's an ideal treatment for tired or dry skin, as it contains many of the oils lost through everyday life.

4 tsp wheat germ oil

4 tbsp avocado oil

1¼ cup (25 g) cocoa butter

1 tsp beeswax

½ tsp borax powder

2 tbsp rosewater

10 drops geranium essential oil

5 drops frankincense essential oil

5 drops sandalwood essential oil

Combine the wheat germ and avocado oil in a heat-resistant bowl and place in a saucepan that has been half-filled with water. Heat, adding the cocoa butter and beeswax until the mixture has blended. Dissolve the borax in the rosewater and add to the mixture by stirring all ingredients together. Remove the saucepan from the heat and add the essential oils. Allow to cool before storing.

SUGAR DELIGHT

I discovered the use of sugar as an exfoliator while traveling. This blend is suitable for most skin types; you'll be amazed at how soft and smooth your skin feels afterwards. This recipe is particularly recommended if you suffer from keratosis pilaris, which looks like small red bumps and/or pimple. Although not infectious or catching, it can look a little unsightly. Regular use of this scrub, along with a loofah, should loosen the pores and leave your arms feeling smoother and looking less blotchy.

2½ cups (250 g) white cane sugar

2½ cups (250 g) avocado oil

2 tsp aloe vera gel

2 drops lavender essential oil

2 drops orange essential oil

Combine the ingredients in a bowl. Scoop some of the scrub and massage gently onto your skin for a minute (the scrub will actually tighten onto your skin like a mask). Leave on for 3 to 4 minutes before rinsing. This scrub can be used all over your body.

Warning: Some people develop temporary blotchiness after using this scrub, but it is only temporary. If you don't have the above ingredients, just add sugar to your cleanser for a moisturizing exfoliating scrub for smooth skin.

NUTTY BODY SCRUB

Using natural ingredients such as nuts and oatmeal will not only exfoliate your body without irritating it, but the oil in the nuts will also provide a moisturising film on your skin, so your skin won't dry out. For all skin types, particularly dry.

⅔ cup (100 g) finely ground nuts (try almonds or flax seeds)
½ cup (50 g) oatmeal
½ cup (50 g) whole wheat flour

Blend the ingredients until they are reduced to a coarse mixture. Pour into a glass jar with a screw top. To use, scoop out a handful and place into a bowl, adding water to make a paste. Rub over your body to loosen any dry or flaking skin. Mixture can be stored in a freezer.

MID-WEEK SCRUB

Using grains ensures that you won't experience a sensitive reaction, as they are quite soft on your skin. This recipe is great if you like to exfoliate more than once a week.

2 tbsp oatmeal
2 tbsp cornmeal
2 tbsp wheat germ

Perfect for exfoliating normal to sensitive skin. Mix ingredients together and store in an airtight container. Make a paste by adding warm water to 1 tablespoon of the mixture.

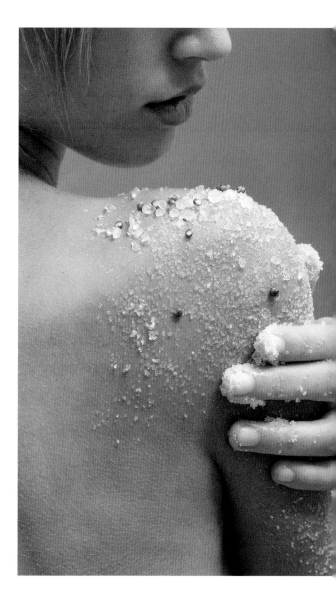

Detox home facial

Spending time at home taking care of yourself can be a pampering treat in itself—imagine the luxury of having the place to yourself. (It happens so rarely that you should cherish every moment.) So go on, unplug the telephone, light some candles, and put on your favorite music. This time is for you and you alone.

BEFORE YOU START

It's important to know your skin type, as this can determine the type of products you should use—to the extent that even certain sunscreens are formulated for various skin types. I would highly recommend that you visit a beauty counter or dermatologist for confirmation. Here's a brief breakdown of the various skin types to help you find out which category your skin fits into:

Dry skin is thin and usually free of blemishes. It can feel tight, particularly after showering or swimming. It can burn or peel easily, in both hot and cold weather. With dry skin you probably have wrinkles around the eyes and mouth, no matter what your age.

Quick test: Press an area on your face hard with your finger and hold it for 15 seconds. Release. If the red spot doesn't disappear for a long time, your skin is most likely dry.

Oily skin often looks shiny and unhealthy because of its greasy appearance and the large, open pores which are a major signifier (especially around the nose and cheek area). You probably already know whether or not you have oily skin, as an unfortunate side effect is that you may have suffered from pimples or acne.

Quick test: Take a clean mirror and press it to your nose, forehead, and cheeks. If you notice greasy prints on the mirror, your skin is oily.

Mixed skin type is the most common. If you are unsure, a normal characteristic is that while the T-zone (nose, forehead, and chin) is oily, the cheeks are dry. One-in-five women have a mixed skin-type.

Normal skin is certainly the most sought-after skin type. You probably suffer very little from blemishes and have only small signs of aging. In fact, you can probably use any beauty product and it doesn't make much of a difference. You are very lucky—most people would kill for this skin type!

Home treatments

The best products you can use on your skin are natural ones. Take a look at any product in your beauty cabinet, and undoubtedly it'll contain vitamins A and E or fruits or vegetables such as pomegranate or carrots. Even green or white tea is utilized for its calming and antiaging properties.

So Mother Nature does know best when it comes to using natural ingredients. The following beauty treatment recipes are designed for either dry, normal, or oily skin (and are marked accordingly) and should last you at least four weeks, unless otherwise stated. Most of the ingredients can be found in your fridge or cupboard, so before you start your detox day, make sure you're stocked up with all you need so that you don't have to run to the store in your pajamas with a face mask on!

CLEANSERS

Cleansers . . . clean the skin. They really do what they say, although most of us only cleanse our skin once a day. When you think of all the dirt and grime our skin is confronted with each day, it's ridiculous that we don't take better care and time to clean away the day every evening. I would recommend cleaning your skin as soon as you get home—that way your skin has the evening to breathe.

When cleansing your skin, make sure to use lukewarm water only—too hot and you risk scalding the top layer, too cool and you may dry it out. Pat the mixture in gently and remove with either organic cotton pads or by splashing water onto your face. Avoid using a facecloth—mainly because these drag your skin, which can encourage the formation of wrinkles.

MILK AND TOMATO JUICE CLEANSER

The high acid content in the recipe—lactic acid in the milk and fruit acid in the tomato—gives this lotion a gentle peeling action. Test on the inside arm or wrist for any possible allergic reactions before using on the face.
Recommended for: *normal and oily skin types*

1 medium very ripe tomato
⅔ cup (150 ml) fresh whole milk
filtered water

Juice or blend the tomato. Strain through a piece of muslin or tea towel, and discard the pulp. Add the tomato juice to an equal amount of fresh milk. Store in a covered container or bottle in the refrigerator. Keep for no longer than five days. Apply to the face and neck, using cotton pads, once or twice a day. Leave on for 10 minutes and rinse with filtered water and pat dry.

YUMMY MUMMY

The cream in this recipe is perfect for restoring moisture to dry skin. Rose oil is also wonderful and calming and can help restore the balance of natural oils in the skin.

1 tbsp heavy dairy cream
2 drops rose essential oil

Combine and use as you would a cleansing lotion. Massage into your skin, using upward strokes, and remove with water or a warm muslin cloth. This cleanser can be used daily. Store in an airtight container in the refrigerator for no longer than three days.

STRAWBERRY STEAMER

Steaming your skin not only brings a healthy glow to your skin, but is ideal for unblocking pores, ideal if you're suffering from repeated breakouts or problem skin. Use at least once a week.

1 tbsp dried lavender
½ cup (50 g) fresh strawberries
1 tbsp red clover leaves (available from
    Chinese herbalists)

Sprinkle the lavender, strawberries, and red clover leaves in a bowl of steaming water. Place your face over the steamy concoction and cover your head with a towel. Leave for 5–15 minutes. Rinse your face with cool water and pat dry.

TONERS

Toners rehydrate, cool, nourish and refresh your skin. They remove any remaining traces of dirt, make-up, or oil that your cleanser may have not dissolved. When purchasing a toner, choose one that doesn't contain alcohol, as this may further dry the skin. Opinion is mixed on whether toners are a necessary part of the cleansing regime. Make up your own mind and experiment. If your skin feels better when you use a toner, then continue to do so. However, if your main reason for using a toner is to cool it down after cleansing, then spritz your skin with water instead.

COOLING TONER FOR SENSITIVE SKIN

Cucumber reduces puffiness and redness. Camomile is also an excellent soothing ingredient—ideal if your skin is super sensitive.
Recommended for: *sensitive skin*

1 cucumber
½ carrot
¼ cup camomile tea
½ cup lemon juice

Juice the cucumber and carrot. Add camomile tea and lemon juice. Combine all the ingredients in a glass jar and shake to blend. Use a cotton wool ball to apply to your face. Keep refrigerated and store for no longer than three days.

EXFOLIATORS

By ridding the skin of dead cells, exfoliating allows new skin cells to emerge. Your appearance will take on a healthier glow and will be more responsive to treatments. Make sure you choose the correct exfoliant for your skin type:

Dry skin: a creamy exfoliant won't irritate the natural oils and sensitive balance of dry skin

Normal skin: as this skin type is more resilient, you can use an exfoliant with small granules in it to remove dead skin cells

Oily skin: use an exfoliant that doesn't contain any irritants, as it may upset the pH balance of the skin and provoke skin eruptions

See page 99 for exfoliator recipes.

FACE MASKS

Face masks tend to be considered indulgent, but in actual fact, they are a necessary part of your skin care regime. While daily cleansing, toning, and moisturizing are a must for clean, glowing skin, it is important to take some time to "rest" and nurture your skin through various and appropriate masks. Aim to apply a face mask at least once a week. After cleansing and exfoliating, the skin on your face has warmed, the pores opened, and it will respond better to a mask.

The type of mask you choose is up to you. Oily skins tend to prefer masks that tighten; dry skins are more suitable to thick, gloopy concoctions; normal skin is lucky enough to choose between the two.

When you apply a mask, make a pampering experience out of it. Run a hot bath, light some candles, and play your favorite music. After applying the mask, soak in the bathtub for at least 10–15 minutes. The heat and steam from the bath will not only work wonders on your stress levels, but they will also encourage your skin to respond positively to the treatment (by opening the pores and relaxing any stress and frown lines). Always apply moisturizer after cleaning off your mask with cold water.

FACE MASK FOR NORMAL SKIN

Egg and lemon combined make an excellent purifying and skin-tightening mask. The lemon in particular will help abolish any problem spots or dry areas. Normal skin can usually handle astringent ingredients such as lemons, and they help to balance the oils in the skin.

1 tbsp whiskey
1 egg
¼ cup (25 g) non-fat dry milk powder
juice of 1 lemon

Combine all the ingredients. Spread the compound over the entire face, avoiding the eye area. Allow to dry. Remove with a wet wash cloth. Use once a week.

FRESH WATERMELON MASK

Watermelon is extremely refreshing and very hydrating for the skin. This recipe is excellent for oily skin. If you have dry skin add a banana instead of yogurt.

1 cup (100 g) watermelon, chopped
3 tbsp yogurt

Mash the watermelon in a small bowl until smooth. Add the yogurt and blend. Apply to the face and neck, and cover your face with a moist cloth. Leave for 10 minutes and rinse with lukewarm water. Rinse dry.

ANTIAGING BANANA MASK

Bananas contain large quantities of magnesium, potassium, iron, zinc, iodine, and vitamins A, B, E, and F. This mask is an ideal antiaging treatment for skin of all ages.

1 small banana
2 tbsp fresh heavy cream
1 tbsp honey (organic if possible)
1 tbsp oat flour
bottled or spring water

Mash the banana, and then add cream, honey, and flour. Mix well. You may need to add more cream or flour to obtain the right consistency. Apply mask to a clean face, making sure you include the area around the eyes and the neck, and leave on for 30 minutes. Rinse off with water and pat dry.

FIRMING MASK

Strawberries help to restore elasticity and vitality to your skin. This recipe is ideal for tired-looking skin.

1¼ cups (125 g) strawberries, very ripe
¾ cup (75 g) cornstarch

Mix strawberries and cornstarch together to make a paste and apply to the face, avoiding the delicate area around your eyes. Leave on for 30 minutes and rinse off with cool water.

BRIGHTEN UP

This face mask will help restore tone and vitality to your skin. Strawberries add color to your skin, as their antioxidants help to fight free radicals, which may rob the skin of its luster. Cucumber is also extremely cooling. This mask is ideal for all skin types. The honey is an excellent healer. You can apply honey directly to spots or scars to help speed up the healing process.

1 tbsp ground almonds
3 strawberries
½ cucumber
1 tsp honey (organic if possible)
1 tbsp yogurt

Blend the ingredients together until smooth. Apply the mixture to cleansed, damp skin. Leave for 15 minutes or until dry. Gently wipe off with a damp wash cloth.

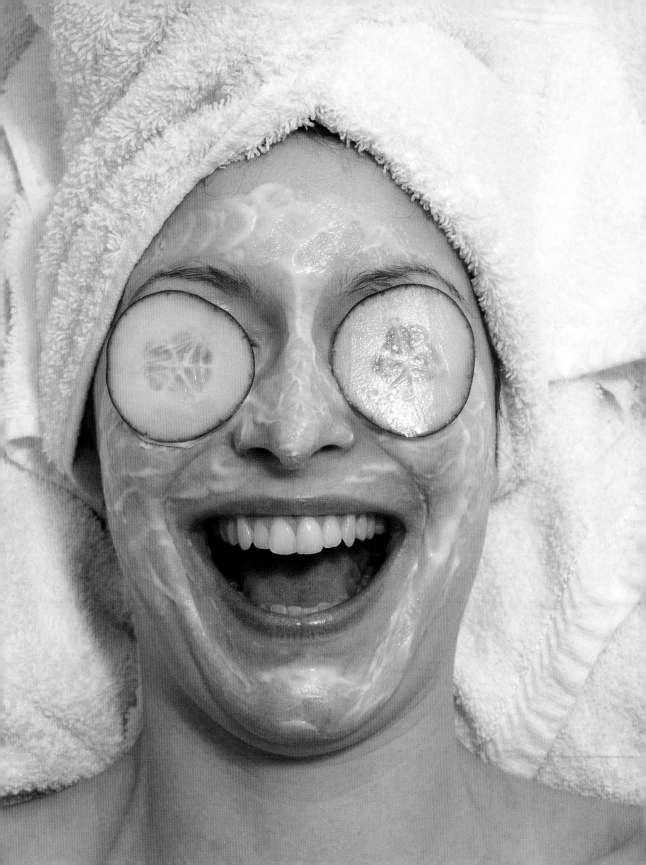

MOISTURIZERS

All skin has its own natural moisturizing factor that regulates water flow from the dermis to the surface. Sebum also helps by forming a barrier on the skin which prevents moisture loss. As we grow older both of these decrease in activity and therefore we need a water-regulating moisturizer to help maintain its previous levels. Moisturizing day and night not only provides your skin with the external hydration it requires, but some moisturizers also provide protection against external factors such as sunlight, pollution, heating, and air-conditioning.

While some beauty therapists recommend a different moisturizer for day and night, most agree that the correct moisturizer should be sufficient for both. However, whatever you choose, make sure that your day cream has an SPF of at least 15+. If it doesn't, then always apply a layer of sun screen before you leave the house.

There's no rule that says you have to use moisturizer all over your face; you may just need a light eye cream and a bit of moisturizer on your drier cheek area.

EVERYDAY MOISTURIZER

Use this cream twice a day after cleansing and toning. Grapefruit has astringent properties which help to tighten pores and refresh tired skin, which helps eliminate dead cells.

1½ cups (150 g) almond oil
1 cup (100 g) cocoa butter
1 tsp royal jelly
¼ cup (25 g) beeswax
10 fl oz (300 ml) distilled water
30 drops grapefruit extract oil
Combine the almond oil, cocoa butter, royal

jelly, and beeswax and melt over a low heat, stirring occasionally. Remove from the stove and add water. Blend until the mixture is thick and creamy. Add the grapefruit oil. Store in glass jars with screw-on tops. This mixture lasts around four months, but you must discard if you notice any discoloration or mold.

THIRSTY SKIN MOISTURIZER

Avocados are extremely high in essential fatty acids—one of the highest sources—which means they're not just good for your diet, they're a fabulous face treatment as well. Combined with the nourishing wheatgerm oil, cocoa butter, and beeswax, this is an ideal moisture replenisher for dry, tired complexions.

4 tsp wheat germ oil
4 tbsp avocado oil
¼ cup (25 g) cocoa butter
1 tsp beeswax
2 tbsp rose water
10 drops geranium essential oil
5 drops frankincense essential oil
5 drops sandalwood essential oil

Combine the wheatgerm and avocado oils in a heat-resistant bowl and place in a pan which has been half-filled with water. Heat, adding the cocoa butter and beeswax until the mixture is blended. Add rose water. Remove from the heat and add the essential oils. Allow to cool before storing in an airtight container. Keep in the refrigerator and discard after one month.

ALL OVER BODY PAMPER

Using essential oils can help hydrate extremely dry skin and return it to its natural moisture level. Camomile not only soothes and calms tired, sensitive skin, but it can also help if you suffer from insomnia. Rosemary and neroli are stimulating and ideal for the body as they also help to relax muscle tension.

10 drops lavender essential oil
10 drops Roman chamomile essential oil
10 drops neroli essential oil
10 drops rosemary essential oil
10 drops carrot seed oil
⅔ cup (60 g) almond, olive, or sesame oil

Apply the oil once a day after bathing or showering while your skin is still damp. This helps your body retain the moisture from bathing, as oil provides an external sealant, trapping moisture and keeping your skin hydrated and smooth. Store in an airtight jar for no longer than four weeks.

HAIR TREATMENT

It's not just your skin that needs regular moisturizing, you should give your hair a weekly treat, too.

LEAVE-IN CONDITIONER

Increase the shine of your hair with these essential oils. The oils work by coating the hair shaft, coaxing the follicles to lie flat. When flat, light is reflected off the hair, creating an illusion of shiny hair. By leaving the oils on your hair overnight, they will have the opportunity to penetrate deeper. If your hair is dry or lifeless, use this treatment once a week and always keep it on overnight.

3 drops neroli oil
3 drops chamomile essential oil
3 drops lavender essential oil
3 drops rosemary essential oil

Mix the ingredients in a small bowl. Shampoo hair as normal. Towel dry and apply the mixture. Comb through and allow to dry naturally. Discard any excess mixture.

Sauna/steam treatments

Saunas

Go to any gym or health club and chances are that they will have a sauna and/or a steam room. Saunas and steam rooms have been around for years, but recently, these heated rooms have come into their own, with many people realizing the health benefits of sitting in a darkened room, sweating out their toxins.

Relaxing in a heated environment helps to relax your tired muscles, as well as eliminate toxins through your sweat. They're great to visit during your detox, as they'll speed up the elimination process, in a similar manner to intensive exercise. This is because heat increases your circulation, moving blood and oxygen around your body, ultimately increasing the removal of toxins through bodily waste and the skin.

With your blood circulation increased by around 75 percent, of which 70 percent reaches the skin, toxins simply find it easier to leave the body through your pores. As your body heats up, your pores open, and water and toxins escape. Because you lose around 1 fl oz (30 ml) of water during a 10 minute sauna session, it is important to drink filtered water while you're in the room and afterward.

HOW LONG SHOULD I STAY IN?

Short bursts of heat are better than long periods in a sauna, mainly because you'll reduce your chances of becoming dehydrated and drying your skin out. As the air inside is very arid (around 170°F/80°C), there is a danger of drying your skin out too extensively, and also releasing too many toxins from your system. Ideally, stay for no longer than 20 minutes. If 20 minutes in one sitting seems interminable, break it up into 5-minute chunks, and plunge into a cold pool or shower to "shock" your system. Your skin will be glowing and your mind will be extremely awake!

HOW TO PREPARE

Other than taking in a bottle of water to sip during your sauna visit, you should also be aware that you should not eat a heavy meal nor drink alcohol before entering a sauna. I would also suggest avoiding alcohol afterwards. Because your circulation will have speeded up you'll get drunk more quickly.

MEDICAL NOTES

If you're pregnant, have heart problems, diabetes, epilepsy, respiratory problems, or skin problems such as eczema, then avoid saunas unless your family doctor has given you the all clear. If you feel faint or lightheaded or nauseous at any time, leave the sauna immediately.

Steam rooms

A steam room is basically a "wet air room" and many health spas now include aromatherapy oils, such as peppermint, lavender, or eucalyptus oil to help you relax or clear your lungs. I highly recommend a steam room if you find a sauna too drying or you have been suffering from chest colds or flu.

HOW IT WORKS

The wet air infiltrates the lungs and slows the production of bacteria or viruses, which can lead to illnesses. The steam opens up the airways in the lungs, making breathing much easier as the muscles relax their tight hold. Steam rooms that use aromatherapy oils such as tea tree or eucalyptus can also help to accelerate the relaxation process and eliminate bacteria from the bronchioles and nasal cavities.

If you suffer from scaly skin or pustules, steam rooms can help loosen the dead skin. Spend around

3–5 minutes in the steam room, followed by a warm shower. Using a loofah or body scrub (see page 99) gently apply to the affected area. This should loosen the flaky skin and blocked pores, leaving you with smooth, baby-soft skin. Don't rub too hard though, as your skin will be especially sensitive after the heated room.

HOW LONG SHOULD I STAY IN?

As a steam room is less drying than a sauna, it will be tempting to stay in for as long as possible. However, this wet air can be deceptive and you will still be susceptible to dehydration. Stay in no longer than 20 minutes, although shorter bursts are preferable—particularly if interrupted by cold showers or a dip in a plunge pool.

Follow the advice given for using saunas if you suffer from a medical condition or are pregnant.

TIP

Make the most of the warm environment and use the time to pamper yourself. Apply a hair treatment and face mask before you go into the sauna or steam room. The heat will open your pores and hair follicles, which will allow the ingredients of the beauty treatment to soak in and work more effectively. Again, leave the treatment in place no longer than 20 minutes, and if you experience a burning or itching sensation, wash the treatment off immediately.

mind and spirit detox

Ayurveda

More and more health practitioners, therapists, and even spas are now looking to the Eastern world for healing practices, and one that has gained in popularity during the past decade is Ayurveda.

What is Ayurveda?

Unlike many detox treatments, Ayurveda has been around since 3000 BCE. The basis of Ayurveda lies in the balance of three "doshas" in the body. To follow an ayurvedic way of life, it is first necessary to discover which dosha you are.

A lifestyle and nutrition program is then prescribed to help balance the body and mind, and help with the healing process (which may include a strict detoxification if necessary). To help support this, there are also ayurvedic massages and herbal supplements prescribed.

✳ ARE YOU SUFFERING FROM STRESS?

Do you:
• Notice that you have moist palms, feet, or underarms?

• Have indigestion?

• Experience difficulty falling or staying asleep?

• Suffer from asthma or hay fever flare-ups?

• Suffer from constipation or diarrhea?

• Notice that you have a fast pulse?

• Experience shortness of breath?

• Suffer from headaches?

• Have cold hands or feet?

If you agree with three or more of the above questions, then you need to take some time out to help your body recover from the effects of stress. Try one of the alternative relaxation programs outlined in this chapter to help you deal with your stress levels, including Ayurveda, aromatherapy, meditation, flower remedies, and energy work/chakras.

Which dosha are you?

PITTA

Health focus: controls the metabolism and the body's ability to process air, food, and water

Personality: highly-motivated, intelligent. You tend to find it difficult to wind down and like being the center of attention.

Health issues: stress-related illnesses, such as lethargy, overweight or underweight, insomnia, premenstrual syndrome, dry skin, irritable bowel, or poorly functioning bowel.

Detox treatment: The aim for pittas when detoxing is to help them destress and calm their busy minds to help give their bodies a rest as well. Try having a massage at least once a month (ideally one that deals with Ayurvedic health) and make sure that you eat healthy, wholesome meals of fruit and vegetables. Foods that are processed or high in sugar will be difficult for your body to digest, so avoid these where possible. Avoid caffeine, particularly after 3 PM, and try to cut down on alcohol (and cigarettes of course), as these will only over-stimulate you.

KAPHA

Health focus: body and muscle

Personality: kapha types tend to be muscular and have long, lean bodies, as kapha rules the skeleton and structure. Tend to be caring and a "shoulder to cry on" for friends.

Health issues: can suffer from overtiredness, particularly due to putting others' needs first. Muscular aches and pains are common and many kaphas suffer from allergies.

Detox treatment: First try to ensure that your own needs are met (take a look at the Mental Detox Weekend on page 123), and remember to take time out each day for yourself. Epsom salt baths are ideal to help heal sore and aching muscles. Try drinking dandelion tea to eliminate water retention, and eat water-based foods, such as seafood, watermelon, watercress, and tomatoes. Juices are also a great way for you to start the day.

VATA

Health focus: nervous system

Personality: scattered and unpredictable. Moods are irregular, extreme highs and extreme lows. Tend to suffer from insomnia, or have trouble rising from your bed. Inconsistent is the best way to describe you and your health. Very confident and ambitious and tend to work best in a creative environment.

Health issues: depression, hyperactivity, skin problems, especially pimples or acne. Become stressed and anxious very easily.

Detox treatment: The focus for vata types is to help even out mood and energy levels. Follow the Mental Detox Weekend on page 123 to help get into a routine of health and nutrition. Try joining a boxing class to help focus your nervous energy, but don't forget to balance this with yoga or meditation classes. Foods such as spinach, salmon, potatoes, broccoli, and asparagus will help to cleanse and calm your body. Avoid caffeine as much as possible, replacing it with either Ayurvedic teas for your type, or calming teas such as green, white, or mint.

Aromatherapy

Aromatherapy is the use of aromatic essences extracted from plants, and it works by prompting a chemical change in the brain. These extracted oils are the plant hormones—the most vital substance of the plant. Essential oils should never be used directly on the skin—add them to massage oil or cream.

Even some oils (such as lemon) may be too strong to add undiluted to a bath. Take a look at the following essences to see which oil is for you:

Cardamom
Good for: if you're feeling tired, exhausted, or run down
When to use it: winter
How to use it: To ward off colds and flu, mix 4 drops each of rose and tea tree oil with 2 drops of cardamom oil and 1 tsp (5 ml) base oil and add to your bath.

Clary sage
Good for: when you're feeling blue (it also helps to relieve the symptoms of premenstrual syndrome)
When to use it: in the morning
How to use it: Mix 12 drops of clary sage, 10 drops of geranium, and 3 drops of rose oil with 3 ½ tbsp (50 ml) of base carrier oil, and apply in a circular motion to your stomach.

Grapefruit
Good for: preventing hunger pangs and overeating
When to use: whenever you feel the desire to raid the cookie jar
How to use it: Keep some grapefruit oil in your handbag and sniff before a meal. Many celebrities apparently burn grapefruit oil in their homes and sniff a scented tissue in order to keep their figures.

Lavender
Good for: insomnia, and to calm and soothe
When to use it: when you're panicked and stressed (best used at night)
How to use it: Add 4–8 drops to your bath, or put 2 drops on your pillow to help you sleep.

May chang
Good for: increasing energy levels, lifts moods, and beats depression
When to use it: any time you're in need of a lift
How to use it: Put 5–6 drops in an oil burner. Or put 2 drops of may chang and frankincense oil in your bath for an energizing soak.

Rose
Good for: calming
When to use it: bathtime
How to use it: Mix 6 drops of sandalwood, 4 drops of orange, and 1 drop of rose oil with a glass of full-fat milk or base carrier oil into your bath.

Rosemary
Good for: stimulating and invigorating
When to use it: during the day
How to use it: Mix 10 drops with a base carrier oil and rub on your hands and feet to help you think clearly.

Some oils can counteract homeopathic remedies, so be sure to check with a homeopath if you are using both treatments simultaneously.

Meditation

The importance of relaxation

When did you last feel truly relaxed? Chances are that your memory of relaxation is as distant as last year's vacation memories. The reality is that we just don't have the time to relax. Taking time to relax is actually just adding another stressful demand on top of an already towering list of demands.

But taking time to relax is just as important as eating well. A relaxed body can deflect illness and heal quicker than one addled with stress as your body is more likely to have the energy to maintain a strong and healthy immune system. When we are stressed we are more likely to be deficient in essential nutrients, which therefore impacts our health. This is because our body uses our stores of vitamins and minerals to help it cope with stress, leaving less to feed our body.

Breathing for health

It's ironic that the very action we all do, around 30,000 times a day, without prompting or thought, is the very thing that most of us are doing incorrectly. Breathing well is the simplest way to relieve tension in body and mind. A deep breath, one that begins in your stomach and moves up to your chest, puts masses of oxygen into the bloodstream for an instant health boost to the whole body. A few deep breaths will clear your mind, reawaken your brain, and relax your entire body.

How to breathe

Place one hand on your chest and the other on your navel. If the lower hand doesn't move, you're not breathing deeply enough. Forget about flattening your stomach and take in a long, deep breath. As you breathe in, feel your abdomen rise and see the movement parting your fingertips. Whenever you feel stressed or uptight, take a moment to check your breathing. Odds are, you've moved the focus of your breathing back to your chest area, so take the time to correct your breathing technique and enjoy the short break this affords you. Eventually, you will breathe correctly as a matter of course, it just takes a bit of time and practice.

BREATHING EXERCISE

This exercise is best done during the day if you feel that things are getting the better of you. Find a quiet spot to sit comfortably (even if it is your office bathroom) and sit with your back straight. You can sit cross-legged or with your back against a hard wall, as long as your feet are resting comfortably on the floor.

Allow your breathing to slow naturally, don't force it. Place your hands side by side on your abdomen, fingertips meeting just below the navel. Take a deep breath through your nose and feel the oxygen moving into every part of your lungs. Feel your abdomen rise under your fingers. Then breathe out and feel your hands fall with the motion. Repeat this five times, before allowing your body to fall into its natural breathing rhythm.

If you like to concentrate on an affirmation, or positive thought during this process, concentrate on what you believe you need at that moment. For instance, if you are about to go into a difficult meeting, repeat, "I am strong and talented and admired," with each breath. If you're feeling unloved or vulnerable, try the mantra "I am love" with each in breath to create a feeling of love and warmth.

Meditation for health

Just as breathing correctly is extremely important for health and well-being, so daily meditation is also a powerful tool to help control and manage stress. Once a "hippy" pastime, scientists now consider meditation an important part of well-being, as it helps to lower blood pressure, reduce stress, and eliminate fine lines and wrinkles. By taking time out and allowing your body to rest, you're providing it with the opportunity to repair itself and rebuild its energy stores. Meditating for as little as 5 minutes a day can help bring about these health benefits, though for a total mind massage try meditating for 20 minutes whenever possible.

MEDITATION EXERCISE

Sit or lie comfortably. If you are lying down, be careful not to fall asleep! Set a clock for the duration of the meditation, so you don't have to interrupt your peaceful thoughts to check the time. Close your eyes and begin the breathing process (see page 116). Allow your thoughts to release with each exhalation. Some people find it necessary to focus on a word or number so that their minds don't wander. If you prefer, use the simple method of counting. With each out breath, count one, the next breath, two, and so on. Over time your mind will wander, begin at one and start counting again. If you find it impossible to still your mind the moment your eyes close, try this method instead. Light a candle and stare into the center of the flame. Blink whenever necessary and allow your breathing to be calm and steady.

Flower remedies

There is a growing interest in a more subtle use of flowers in remedies and essences. This simple method was first used back in the 1500s by the healer Paracelsus, who prepared remedies from dew collected from flowers to treat his patients' emotional problems.

The theory and technique was rediscovered by Dr. Edward Bach, a respected physician and researcher living in the United Kingdom towards the end of the nineteenth century.

Flower remedies are useful in dealing with a number of conditions. They work by stimulating the body's own capacity to heal itself by balancing negative feelings, helping you to take control, to recover from shock or upset, and kick-start your motivation—whether it's to break a bad habit or turn over a new leaf. There are several types of flower remedies—Bach, Australian Bush Flower, Californian—to name just a few. Ideally, visit a healer who will either make you a bespoke remedy or recommend an all-encompassing remedy.

How to choose your remedy

There are literally thousands of flower remedies to choose from, each with its own unique properties, so at first it can appear impossible to pick one that is suitable. This is where a practitioner can help determine which is best for you.

HOW TO TAKE YOUR REMEDY

You take flower essences by dotting them onto your tongue or by drinking a few drops in a glass of water.

Energy work and chakras

If you're constantly feeling tired, run down, and emotional (and your family doctor has already tested you for all the usual suspects), it may be that your chakras are out of line. This alternative form of treatment can help to address what is tiring you out. Energy and chakra work include methods such as acupressure, breathing, visualization, massage, and acupuncture.

What are chakras?

We all have seven chakra points in our body: the top of the head, between the eyebrows (also known as the "third eye"), the throat, chest, above and below the navel, and the base of the spine. Chakras are believed to be the energy centers of the body, and each chakra "vibrates" at a different color (see image on page 122). By keeping all seven chakras vibrating at their optimum level, it is believed that you can ward off bad health, or even lessen the effects of illness. This is because chakras are thought to be connected to our nervous system and endocrine system—if they are aligned then the rest of our body works in harmony. If they're out of whack, or there is a "blockage," then the body is unable to circulate energy effectively. Numerous studies around the world have found that chakra can be effective in treatments such as depression, fibromyalgia, thyroid, and even some cancers. (If you intend to try chakra rebalancing for illnesses such as cancer, it's important that you inform your medical team first.)

THE CHAKRAS

THE ROOT CHAKRA
Color: red
Area: base of spine/anus
Associated with: security, trust, and ability to function within everyday issues
Problems: weight issues, lethargic, apathetic, constipation
Everyday solutions: Eat plenty of fibrous foods and exercise regularly. It's also important to keep your system hydrated to flush out toxins.

THE SACRAL CHAKRA
Color: orange
Area: below the navel
Associated with: sexuality, maternal or paternal instincts, happiness
Problems: panic attacks, sexual problems, stomach bugs and cramping (premenstrual syndrome for women), urine infections
Everyday solutions: Eat an alkaline diet and spend some time each day in quiet meditation. This area may benefit from emotional acupuncture treatments, particularly if there is an issue surrounding sexual problems or trauma.

SOLAR PLEXUS CHAKRA
Color: yellow
Area: above the navel
Associated with: self-awareness, ambition and empathy
Problems: allergies, tiredness, muscles, and diabetes
Everyday solutions: Focus on a diet that helps

to calm your nervous system. Stay away from stimulants. A range of activities that help to channel your nervous energy, such as boxing, should be balanced with yoga or meditation.

HEART CHAKRA

Color: green
Area: heart and chest
Associated with: self-esteem, love, forgiveness, and friendship
Problems: immune problems, such as glandular fever, Epidemic Neuromyasthenia, fatigue, and repetitive colds and flu
Everyday solutions: Focus on a diet that supports and boosts your immune system. During busy times take a multivitamin. Regular massages or treatments will help nurture your loving side.

THROAT CHAKRA

Color: blue
Area: throat, neck, ears, and shoulders
Associated with: communication, expressing emotions, and creativity
Problems: sore throat, skeletal problems with the shoulders, arms and hands, asthma, and thyroid problems
Everyday solutions: Drink warm boiled water with lemon, ginger, and honey every morning to keep your throat clear and supple. Avoid sitting at your desk for longer than 20 minutes without a break. Swimming is ideal to keep your upper body strong and flexible. Avoid mucus-forming foods such as dairy, as these can aggravate asthma.

THIRD EYE CHAKRA

Color: indigo
Area: between the eyebrows
Associated with: intuition, thought, and dreams
Problems: headaches, vision problems, and mood swings
Everyday solutions: Drink plenty of filtered water each day (around 4 pints (2 liters)) and eat energy giving fruit and vegetables. Avoid too much red meat; focus on your omega-3s, such as seafood, instead. Focus-based exercises such as rock climbing are ideal to help you center your mind. Tai chi will also help you tap into the intuitive, right side of the brain.

CROWN CHAKRA

Color: purple
Area: top of the head
Associated with: happiness and links to a "higher power"
Problems: epilepsy, multiple sclerosis, extreme fatigue, self-doubt
Everyday solutions: Try the Mental Detox Weekend (page 123)—this can help clear your mind and body before attempting new adventures. Life coaching may also be of help to focus attention.

How can I tell if my chakras need rebalancing?

When all your chakras are in alignment you tend to feel on top of the world, as though nothing will bother you. People will comment on how well you look, and you'll always choose the fastest line in the store. But when your chakras are misaligned, you tend to feel achy, irritable, and that you are having a generally bad day.

THE TREATMENT

A chakra/energy balancing treatment can take many forms. But typically, after a health assessment, you'll lie on a massage table with your eyes closed. The practitioner may use acupuncture needles (for emotional chakra rebalancing), crystals, or touch as part of the session. The focus is on the breathing and visual exercises. For instance, if your throat chakra, which represents the communication area, is blocked, you may be asked to breathe bright blue light into this area. (The throat area is represented by blue—see chart on pages 120–121). You're usually left alone for 20 minutes or so to focus on breathing, or in some instance, an image. Afterwards you'll feel slightly woozy, although refreshed as though you've had a good night's sleep. It is important that you abstain from alcohol or stimulants afterwards. I would suggest booking a treatment when you know you can go straight home to have a hot bath and continue relaxing.

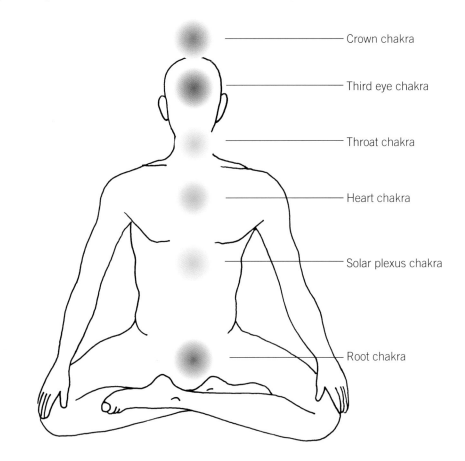

Crown chakra

Third eye chakra

Throat chakra

Heart chakra

Solar plexus chakra

Root chakra

Mental detox weekend

You've been so busy burning the candle at both ends that it's been months since you had a few nights in with just the TV and a 9 o'clock curfew to keep you company. What you need more than anything is not a strict regime of eliminating foods, but a strict diet of "me time."

This weekend program is designed to help you relax, destress, and help banish any worries or fears that may have been lurking for some time.

Preparation

- Turn off your cell phone, computer, and answering machine. It's just two days—people can wait until Monday to speak to you.
- Make sure you have enough healthy food to get you through the weekend.
- Take a peek at the Beauty Boost plan on page 88 to help you relax and make the most of your pampering time.

Day One
MORNING STRETCH
Spend 10 minutes stretching (see page 82 for a stretching routine) to lift your spirits and clear your mind and body of any niggling stresses.

BREAKFAST

ULTIMATE STRESS BUSTER CEREAL
Porridge is believed to not only help banish the blues, keep weight down, and shrink your waistline, but it also helps lower your stress levels.

½ cup (50 g) oatmeal
½ cup (50 g) oat bran flakes
2 tbsp plain natural organic yogurt
1 tbsp ground seeds
   (such as pumpkin and sunflower seeds)
blueberries, strawberries, raspberries,
   or goji berries

Cover oats and flakes with water and leave overnight. Add the yogurt to the porridge and add berries and seeds to taste.

LUNCH

✳ MIXED BEAN SALAD

Beans are packed full of vitamin B and iron, which help your body deal with stress.

4 cups (400 g) mixed beans (try garbanzo
    beans, haricot, or flageolet beans)
lettuce leaves, such as cos, watercress, or arugula
½ apple, cubed
1 heaped tbsp flat leaf parsley and chives
1 tsp olive oil
juice of ½ lemon
1 stick celery, finely chopped
black pepper

Combine all ingredients and serve.

DINNER

✳ SQUASH SOUP

1 tbsp olive oil
1 large onion, finely chopped
2 cloves garlic, crushed
2 large butternut squash, deseeded, peeled,
    and diced
1½ tsp cumin
1 tsp dried cilantro
½ tsp ground nutmeg
¼ tsp chili powder
1 tsp fresh thyme, chopped
3 vegetable stock cubes dissolved in 3 ¾ cups
    (880 ml) hot water
fresh parsley and chives

Heat the oil in a large saucepan. Add the onion and garlic and cook over a low heat until the onion has softened. Add the squash, cumin, cilantro, nutmeg, chili, thyme, and stock. Bring to a boil, reduce heat, and simmer for 15 minutes. Season to taste and add the herbs.

Day Two
BREAKFAST

✳ TASTY MORNING JUICE

The oats and banana in this drink work to help soothe frazzled nerves.

1 cup (250 ml) organic milk
1 banana
1 tbsp muesli
1 tsp Manuka honey
1 tbsp sunflower and pumpkin seeds
nutmeg shavings

Blend all ingredients until smooth. Add ice to chill and drink immediately.

LUNCH

✳ SCRUMPTIOUS SANDWICH

This tasty sandwich is filling and helps to balance out your blood sugar levels. Add any combination of ingredients you like.

2 slices of gluten-free bread
organic chicken pieces
watercress or lettuce leaves
cottage cheese
lemon juice
tomato, sliced
OR
Salmon and cream cheese on toasted soda bread. Garnish with parsley or chives.

DINNER

✳ BROILED SALMON STEAKS

1 salmon steak
1 tsp soy sauce
1 tbsp sesame seeds
black pepper to taste
5 oz (150 g) spinach leaves
5 oz (150 g) tomatoes (or around 3 large
    tomatoes)
2 tbsp (10 g) dairy-free Parmesan cheese
balsamic vinegar dressing

Marinate the salmon in the soy sauce, with
pepper to taste, for about 20 minutes. Add sesame
seeds. Broil the salmon until cooked thoroughly.
Serve on a bed of spinach leaves and tomatoes,
with Parmesan and a balsamic vinegar dressing.

Mind detox tasks

Write down what you'd like to achieve from these next
two days. If you have been stressed about work,
perhaps you can spend some time considering how
to delegate more; or if you've been too busy to begin
a relationship, work out how to start dating again.
Whatever your problem or issue, write down as many
possible solutions as you can. This weekend isn't
about doing, it's about thinking your life through and
writing down your new life plan in black and white.

MIND CLEARING EXERCISE

Find a quiet, comfortable place to sit. Place your
cupped hands over your eyes, then close your eyes.
Take a deep breath and concentrate on allowing the
stresses and strains to leave your body. Hold this
position for at least ten breaths, then remove your
hands from your eyes. Slowly open your eyes and

focus on your surroundings. Remain seated
comfortably for a few more minutes enjoying the
feeling of peacefulness.

ESSENTIAL OILS

Fill an oil burner with boiled water and add 9 drops
of Melissa oil. Melissa essential oil helps to boost the
emotions. Light a tealight and enjoy the refreshing
smell. (For more essential oils see page 114).

WALKING MEDITATION

Walk for at least two hours each day during your mind
detox weekend. Head to a park, and aim to finish at
your favorite café for a cup of peppermint tea and
cake. Walking has been found to be just as effective
as antidepressants when it comes to lifting
depression, and can be an excellent mind clearer.
There's no need to rush, just take your time to enjoy
the sights, sounds, and smells of your environment.

FOOT FETISH

Before you go to bed, give yourself a foot massage.
Hold the area between your first and second toe and
gently press and release ten times. This will stimulate
your stress glands, releasing any pent-up emotion.

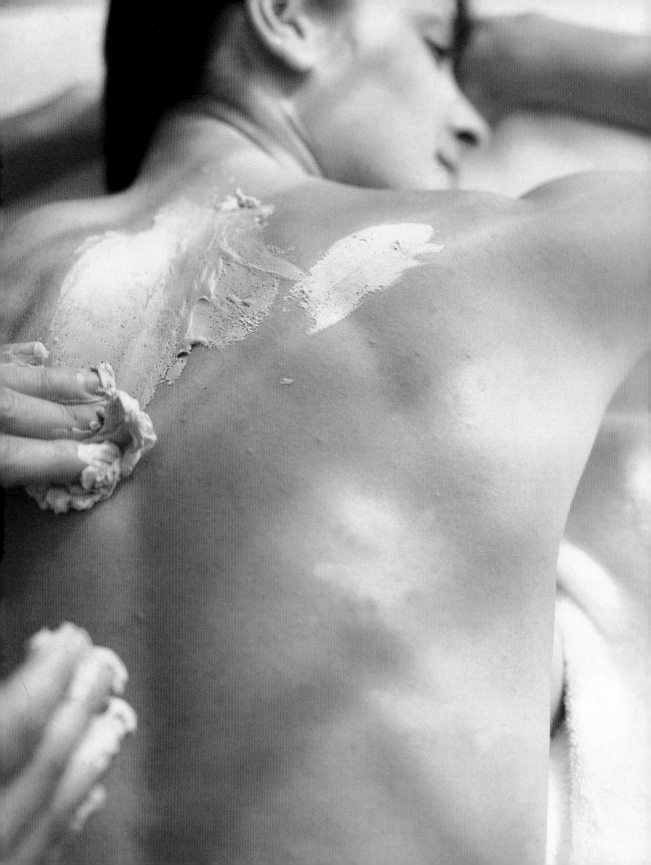

clinic treatments

Spa detox basics

Going to a spa is a treat for all the senses. Even a day spa can feel like a week if it's the right environment and you've booked yourself some treatments.

Before your spa detox

Avoid all alcohol, cigarettes, and coffee at least a day before (ideally, this would be three days, to help eliminate cravings). Avoid eating a heavy breakfast the morning of your visit: some treatments can trigger bowel movements (such as reflexology), so keep this in mind when preparing your prior meals. Shave your legs at least the day before if you are intending on having a massage.

What to take

Most spas provide you with a robe and slippers, and even shampoos and moisturizers, but it's a good idea to check prior to arriving. Remember to pack a brush, a good book or some magazines, and some dried fruits. If you're staying overnight or for a few days, some of your favorite, comforting things could be brought, such as a picture, throw, or pillow. But don't overdo it on the clothes—most of the time you'll be in a robe, so pack comfortable clothes, such as those you'd wear to a yoga class.

The consultation

Before you have any treatment at a spa, you will have a short consultation with a therapist, to determine any health problems as well as your goals and needs during your stay. If you have any type of medical condition, particularly allergies or heart problems, tell the therapist.

Before your treatment

Make sure you arrive in plenty of time for your treatments: your spa visit is all about relaxation, not rushing around. Plus, if you're late for your treatment, your session will be cut short so as not to infringe on the next customer's appointment.

Tell your therapist what you do, or do not like during a treatment. If you prefer the therapist to keep silent throughout the treatment, then let him or her know. They won't be offended! Also let them know whether the pressure of a massage is too hard or too soft. Remember, this is your treatment and the last thing you want is to wake up tomorrow with sore, aching limbs because you were too timid to tell the therapist they were being a little too strong.

After your treatment

Try to take some time to enjoy the feeling of relaxation and bliss after your treatment. There's nothing worse than rushing out into the cold or bustling world after being sequestered in a calm, serene environment all day. Ideally book a taxi, or organize your partner or a friend to collect you from the spa, as you may be too drowsy to drive, plus you'll be able to remain in your pampered world a little longer.

Drink plenty of water afterwards—ideally freshened with lemon or mint, to help the detoxification process. Do ask your therapist for advice on what you should eat afterwards—hot, spicy foods, alcohol, and caffeine are definite no-nos, but some foods, such as warming winter soups may help the healing process of your treatment.

Thalassotherapy

If you've ever spent time in a spa or a Jacuzzi, then you've experienced a form of thalassotherapy. Originating in France, this "water therapy" is designed to help relax the body, while treating conditions such as arthritis, cellulite, asthma, and, of course, toxicity.

Unlike many other treatments in this book, thalassotherapy is a treatment that you can only experience at a beauty salon or, more popularly, a health spa.

If you're at a health spa, hydro or thalassotherapy will be a large part of their detox treatment, as it tends to combine massage, detox, and skin treatments, all in the one appointment. Many spas also suggest hydro and thalassotherapy as a way to end each day, such are their relaxing properties.

According to Champney's Health Spa in the UK, perhaps the most popular spa when it comes to detoxing and treating guests with water therapy, is thalassotherapy—used for beautifying and health-restoring benefits.

What happens during a treatment?

You will usually be given some paper pants to wear, so as not to ruin your swimsuit and be asked to strip down. As you'll be in the pool by yourself, there's no need to worry about your modesty, although you can always insist on wearing your own tops and bottoms.

You'll be instructed to immerse yourself into the warm, purified seawater in the pool and then to relax. The seawater contains minerals that help detoxify as well as smooth the skin. The jets in the pool will pummel the body. This is believed to break down cellulite, boost circulation, and tone tired muscles. Many people find that their aches and pains are soothed immensely after just a 20-minute treatment.

Following this, you may receive a body wrap treatment, which helps to continue to draw out toxins and soothe the body.

WOULD THALASSOTHERAPY BE GOOD FOR ME?

You may benefit from this treatment if you suffer from any of the following symptoms.

- cellulite
- asthma
- psoriasis
- eczema
- arthritis
- aching bones and joints
- if you want to kick-start your detox program

Naturopathic spa program

What is naturopathy?

Naturopathy combines alternative and complementary medicines to treat the mind, body, and soul. Meaning "natural medicine," its foundations originate from Austria and Germany, where treatments have historically embraced an all-encompassing approach.

Like all treatments in this section, the focus is on holistic treatments to treat or cure a specific health problem, while addressing other, underlying health issues. This is because practitioners believe that no health problem is individual—each part of the body relates to another. For instance, spots on the chin may not just be caused by late nights and junk food, but by your bowel's inability to process foods.

How does a naturopathic treatment work?

To follow a naturopathic spa treatment successfully, you will need to visit a qualified practitioner for a health assessment. After this, the naturopath will apply the principles of various therapies to help your healing process, including massage, Ayurveda, nutrition, acupuncture, and herbal treatments.

You'll be asked a series of questions about the following areas of your life, to help determine the state of your health:

- medical history
- lifestyle (working hours, stress levels)
- dietary habits
- sleeping patterns (particularly if these have changed recently)
- bowel movements
- menstrual cycle (regularity, pain, heaviness)

Further tests may also include:

- blood tests
- urine sample
- x-ray
- complete medical check

All these tests will help the practitioner determine the best course of treatment for you, as there are several alternative and complementary forms of remedies to choose from (see the remedies and therapies in the following pages of this chapter).

WOULD NATUROPATHY BE GOOD FOR ME?

If you suffer from any of the following and you've also consulted your doctor or family doctor, then I'd highly recommend visiting a naturopath.

- recurring colds and flu
- skin conditions such as eczema or dermatitis
- asthma
- diarrhea or constipation
- constant tiredness
- bloating or other stomach disorders
- premenstrual syndrome
- chronic fatigue
- Myalgic encephalomyelitis (ME)
- depression
- high or low blood pressure

This list isn't exhaustive: if you feel that you could benefit from a holistic tuning of your health, then a visit to a naturopathic therapist could be just what the doctor ordered.

Homeopathic spa

Homeopathy is unlike most other medicines or alternative treatments. Instead of treating the physical or emotional problem with an opposite (back pain with massage, colds and flu's with medicinal cures), homeopathy actually treats like with like.

How does this work?

Although it's not fully understood how homeopathy works, it has been used for treating illness for hundreds of years. During the 1800s it was used to treat serious illnesses such as scarlet fever, cholera, and yellow fever, and there has also been some success using it to treat animals.

Homeopathy is the treatment whereby the patient is given small amounts in "sugar pill form" of the ailment in the belief that the body will kick-start itself into fighting the infection. As homeopathy means "similar suffering" in Greek, the foundations of it are based on the body's self-healing powers.

For instance, if you are afflicted by hay fever, you will be given tiny quantities of pollen, which would normally induce a sneezing fit. But instead, the body is "reminded" to fight back and increase its defense against such an invasion.

A homeopathic pill is made up of the active ingredient, diluted several times, and a "carrier" substance, usually sucrose. The strength or potency of a pill is described with the letter "c." If the remedy says 100c on the label, this is stronger than one that says 6c. This is because the stronger the remedy, the more it has to be diluted. If you see an "x" on the label, this indicates a weaker potency. Homoeopathy is completely safe, and does not interfere with any other medicines. It's ideal for young children, and even animals.

How to take homeopathic remedies

When taking a remedy, avoid touching it with your fingers, as this can destroy the potency. Instead, tip the small, white pill first into the lid of the bottle and then place it under the tongue where it will dissolve. Don't eat anything 20 minutes before or after taking the remedy.

The following remedies and dosages are recommended for those doing a detox, although ideally, you should visit a homeopath for a consultation. You may then be given dietary changes to help aid your emotional healing. Also, packaged homeopathic remedies are more of a "one stop shop," whereas a practitioner will make up a bespoke remedy for your needs.

NUX VOMICA

Better known for treating hangovers, it's perhaps fitting that this remedy is also ideal for supporting a detox.

Dosage: take one 6c or 30x strength tablet per day for five days (you should begin with the weaker dose and if there is no response, try the stronger one).

SULFUR

Also helps to support the patient during periods of toxicity.

Dosage: take one 6c or 30x strength tablet per day for five days (again, begin with the weaker dose and if there is no response, try the stronger one).

TISSUE SALTS

This is also a form of homeopathy, which takes nutrition into consideration as well. Tissue salts are weaker versions of various other homeopathic remedies, but remain truer to their original substance (most homeopathic remedies contain a similar substance to the original). Tissue salts are based on the believed 12 different salts required by the body for optimum health and functionality. Homeopathic practitioners believe that a lack of one or more of these salts can lead to ill health. Look for combination B tissue salts on the label, which

are specifically for nervous exhaustion and general debility. Take four tablets, three times a day, or every half hour.

Detox programs

There are some homeopathic detox systems available through health food stores and online, but as these are general, fixed treatments, I'd highly recommend you visit a registered practitioner to get advice on homepathic remedies that are tailored to your specific needs. After all, what works for others may not necessarily be the best form of treatment for you.

Detox therapies

Crenotherapy

WHAT IS IT?

An age-old therapy, crenotherapy incorporates mineral water, mud, and steam vapor to increase the health and functionality of the kidneys, stomach, bowels, and liver.

HOW IT WORKS

Crenotherapy uses mineral water, which contains selenium, calcium, and copper—you either drink it to help cleanse out your system, or submerge your body into external therapies, such as Jacuzzis, water massage, or mud treatments. Many European spas offer this treatment and devotees swear by its ability to detox the system, encourage weight loss, and banish cellulite. The minerals in the water help to stimulate the body's natural detoxification system and encourage the elimination of waste. If you don't have access to crenotherapy, then you can also try using a Jacuzzi or place Epsom salts into your bath on a regular basis. Some health spas in Europe suggest the imbibing of Epsom salts, but only do so on the advice and direction of a nutritionist or health professional.

Iridology

WHAT IS IT?

Eyes are the windows to our soul, and also our health it seems. Iridologists believe that your iris (the colored area of the eye) is divided into 12 sections, which correspond to a specific area of the body. Certain color changes, blurriness, or spots in the iris can indicate health problems in the kidneys, stomach, gall bladder, or liver. A whitish circle around the iris can indicate an over-acidic diet, while brown dots within the iris can indicate that your bowel is sluggish.

HOW IT WORKS

By pinpointing areas of weakness, your iridologist can suggest health solutions, although it is usually best to discuss these first with your doctor. If your kidneys or liver aren't functioning at 100 percent optimum health, your iridologist may suggest supplements or change in diet to help cleanse them. Iridology is best used as a recommendation for other treatments, since it only diagnoses ill health. Some iridologists are also trained in other alternative therapies, which means they can help to support their diagnoses with treatments such as homeopathy, acupuncture, or massage.

Colonic irrigation

WHAT IS IT?

Aims to cleanse and promote health in the large bowel. Flushes out feces, undigested foods, and toxins from the large intestine.

HOW IT WORKS

A tube is inserted into the anus and warm water is pumped through, into the intestine. This is meant to rid the intestine of old, unhealthy matter, to allow the bowel to work more productively. Some schools of thought believe that colonic irrigations can cause more harm than good, as they rid the bowel of the "good" bacteria, as well as the bad. If you do decide to try a colonic, ensure that your practitioner is registered and that you follow up your treatment with a course of probiotics to help rebalance the bacteria in your gut. If you're unsure of whether a colonic is for you, then try an alternative, such as the 3-Day Total Detox plan, which is designed to help cleanse the bowel. Drinking warm water every morning with fresh lemon juice can also be effective for your kidney and liver health, and doesn't have the potential harmful side effects of a colonic.

Applied kinesiology
WHAT IS IT?
Kinesiology believes that organ weakness or ill health manifests itself as muscle weakness.

HOW IT WORKS
This has echoes of a magician's trick about it, although many people swear by the accuracy of applied kinesiology. It works by placing samples of food under the patient's tongue, or in a glass container in their hand. The patient is then asked to push their free arm against that of the applied kinesiologist. If the patient finds this difficult, it indicates an allergic or weak response by the body. Once the areas of weakness are identified, the practitioner may suggest a change in diet, some supplements to take, or even exercise to take up (such as yoga or swimming). This form of therapy may require several visits to track your progress and chart how your body is responding to the changes made to your diet and lifestyle.

Light therapy
WHAT IS IT?
Using infra-red light, light therapy is believed to help anything from acne to cancer, arthritis to Seasonal Affective Disorder (SAD).

HOW IT WORKS
Depending on the type of therapy you try, you may be treated using a handheld laser, or a desk-top light box. However, for detoxification purposes, many practitioners use a type of "foot spa," which pulses electric light through the feet to encourage the detoxification process. This is similar in many ways to reflexology; it pinpoints the corresponding bowel, kidney, and liver areas. You rest your feet in the spa for around 30–40 minutes, during which time the water will turn a murky brown, depending on the amount drawn out through the detoxification process. You may feel immensely tired after a treatment, and it's recommended that you do not drink alcohol or eat a heavy meal afterwards. During the past few years, detox foot patches have been launched on the market, which also promise to draw out toxins through the feet.

Space clearing
WHAT IS IT?
If your environment is messy, then it stands to reason that your mind and body are full of rubbish too. Space clearing is similar to Feng Shui, the Chinese belief of how buildings and furniture placement can affect health, wealth and happiness. But space clearing—a Balinese ritual—eliminates any negativity in a building and its atmosphere. Space clearers believe that energy—and even moods—can be stored in the furniture, walls, and floors of a building. If there's too much negative energy stored in a building, this can affect those living in it.

HOW IT WORKS
The space clearing practitioner will light incense, ring bells, and use colored scarves to stimulate healing. The building owners will then be encouraged to clear out junk and even more furniture to help encourage a positive flow of energy. It may sound a bit hippy trippy, but a good clear out of junk and unwanted items is always good for the mind and body. See the 24-Hour Detox Plan (pages 42–46) for tips on how to cleanse your living space for health-giving purposes.

Cranial sacral therapy
WHAT IS IT?

A non-intrusive, but extremely effective treatment, cranial sacral therapy (CST) aims to improve the flow of spinal fluid through the body. If your spine is well aligned, your body and mind will also be healthy and balanced. CST can treat a range of ailments such as muscle pain, insomnia, tiredness, Epstein Barr syndrome, attention deficit hyperactivity disorder (ADHD), premenstrual tension, depression, and post-traumatic shock. It is especially recommended for young babies following a traumatic delivery or those suffering from colic.

HOW IT WORKS

Practitioners place their hands on specific parts of the body, including the skull and sacrum (the base of the spine), and detect patterns of tissue congestion. The practitioner's hands tend to heat up, as the energy flows from them through the client. The treatment may feel ineffectual at first, as there's no manipulation of the body, but it's intensely relaxing and results tend to occur within 24 hours. Many ailments can be treated within a couple of visits (although it does of course depend on the illness), that makes CST an affordable therapy for many.

Marma therapy
WHAT IS IT?

Marmas are the energy areas within the body: similar to chakras, reflexology points, or meridians. This combination of Ayurvedic, yogic, and Chinese medicine means that, as with those therapies, Marma therapy believes that a blockage in a physical area of the body can relate to an emotional one.

HOW IT WORKS

After a consultation with your practitioner, your body will be "scanned" to reveal any blockages. Massage, acupressure, or specific oils can help to treat blockages or stimulate certain areas. For instance, a facial point marma massage will stimulate the mind and help to balance negative thought.

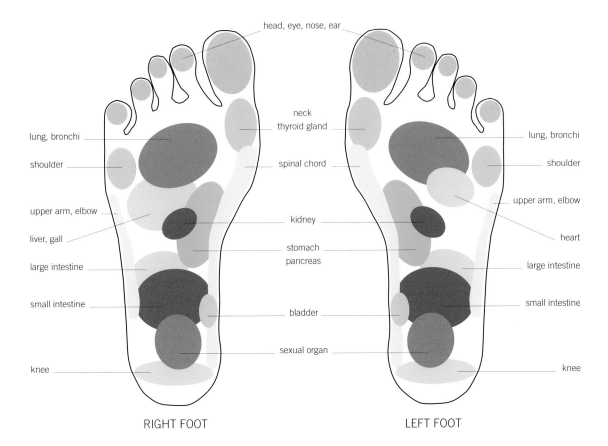

head, eye, nose, ear

neck
thyroid gland

lung, bronchi

shoulder

spinal chord

upper arm, elbow

liver, gall

kidney

large intestine

stomach
pancreas

small intestine

bladder

knee

sexual organ

lung, bronchi

shoulder

upper arm, elbow

heart

large intestine

small intestine

knee

RIGHT FOOT   LEFT FOOT

Reflexology
WHAT IS IT?
Reflexology works by massaging the feet, which are seen as a reflection of the body. For instance, the toes represent the head and neck area, the arch of the foot, your bowel and kidneys. By manipulating these areas, it is possible to promote healing in the corresponding area. It's much less intrusive than say, a direct massage to your head if you have a headache. Reflexology can be great when used as a self-diagnosis tool. By pressing various points of the body, by pinpointing the areas which are tender or sensitive and finding out their related body area, you can diagnose areas which may need support. For instance, if the arch of your foot is particularly sore and tender, this can indicate that your liver is overtired and could benefit from a detox or that you've been overdoing the red wine! A reflexologist is of course more qualified to discover your "weak spots" but a daily foot massage (which can be done by yourself, or somebody else if you're lucky), can be an easy, inexpensive way to chart your overall health.

HOW IT WORKS
A course of reflexology will help to balance the systems of the body, particularly the liver and kidneys, promoting the elimination of toxins, reducing stress and therefore enhancing the body's natural ability to heal itself on all levels. Remember, reflexology can be immensely powerful, particularly when detoxing, so it's important you see a qualified practitioner.

Oxygen therapy

WHAT IS IT?

Why pay for something you get for free? Well, oxygen therapy isn't just about the air around us; it's about specially filtered oxygen fed to you at higher doses. A study at the Human Cognitive Neuroscience Unit of the University of Northumbria found that our brains could function 20 percent better with extra supplies of oxygen. It's ideal for cleansing the system (particularly after a hangover), boosting energy levels, and mental alertness.

HOW IT WORKS

There are various ways to get your extra O_2. You can either inhale through a mask (there are oxygen bars or some gyms have special oxygen rooms for optimum training), or in a sauna-type treatment room which pumps oxygen into the air and ultimately your body. One such therapy, the O2LIVE oxygen system, works by drawing in air, which contains 21 percent oxygen, 78 percent nitrogen, and 1 percent other gases, filtering out the impurities through molecular sieve beds and pumping out up to 95 percent pure filtered oxygen. You place a mask, or use a straw-like tube, to breathe in the oxygen for around 10 minutes (depending on your physical needs). If you are using oxygen therapy for detoxification it's important to follow your practitioner's guidelines and advice.

Reiki

WHAT IS IT?

Reiki (pronounced ray-kee) is a therapeutic technique in which healing energy is channelled from the practitioner into the person receiving the treatment. The name Reiki comes from the Japanese "rei," meaning universal, and "ki," meaning "energy." When ki is blocked, it is believed that sickness and depression can develop.

HOW IT WORKS

If you're feeling low in energy (particularly at the start of a detox program), reiki can help rebalance your levels. By rebalancing your levels it's believed that your body will self-heal by eliminating toxins. A reiki massage is immensely relaxing and is a great treat whether you're detoxing or not! A relaxing massage can help to lower stress levels, increase immunity, and even ward off illness. Try and have a massage at least once a month as part of your health maintenance program.

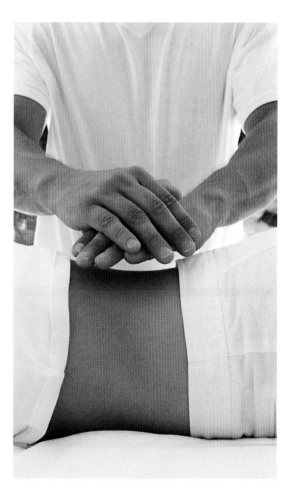

Index

PICTURE CREDITS

The publishers would like to thank the following for permission to reproduce images:

Corbis: 44

Getty images:2, 5, 6, 8, 10, 15, 28, 34, 36, 39, 40, 43, 44, 48, 50, 54, 64, 71, 88, 91, 93, 101, 109, 110, 119, 126, 129, 130, 131, 134, 139

iStock Photo: 12, 14, 16, 17, 19, 22, 27, 30, 33, 35, 36, 38, 42, 47, 52, 53, 57, 58, 61, 67, 73, 75, 77, 78, 85, 90, 98, 101, 107, 117, 123, 133

Photolibrary: 24, 26, 86, 97, 99, 105, 112, 118, 137